KV-117-360

DARTNELL'S PROFESSIONAL SELLING SERIES

VOLUME 1

MORE THAN A FOOT IN THE DOOR

THE SALES PROFESSIONAL'S GUIDE TO WINNING NEW ACCOUNTS

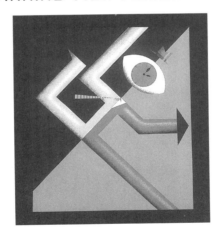

COMPILED BY THE
EDITORS AT DARTNELL

ILLUSTRATIONS: TERRY ALLEN

Dartnell is a publisher serving the world of business with book manuals, newsletters and bulletins, and training materials for executives, managers, supervisors, salespeople, financial officers, personnel executives, and office employees. Dartnell also produces management and sales training videos and audiocassettes and publishes many useful business forms, and many of its materials and films are available in languages other than English. Dartnell, established in 1917, serves the world's business community. For details, catalogs, and product information write:

THE DARTNELL CORPORATION
4660 N Ravenswood Ave
Chicago, IL 60640-4595, U.S.A.
or phone (800) 621-5463 in U.S. and Canada

Dartnell Training Limited
125 High Holborn
London, England
WCLV 6QA
or phone 011-44-071-404-1585

Copyright ©1995
in the United States and Canada
THE DARTNELL CORPORATION
Library of Congress Catalog Card Number: 95-68837
ISBN 0-85013-239-8

Printed in the United States of America

CONTRIBUTORS

Jim Rapp
The Rapp Group Inc.
Alexandria, Virginia

Hal Fahner
Jacksonville Beach, Florida

Brad Goldstein
Skokie, Illinois

John L. Harris
Hickory, North Carolina

Bob Newzell
GCL Associates
Wheeling, Illinois

Robert Taylor
Sales Counselors
Glenview, Illinois

Vicki Dellacecca
Chicago, IL

Richard Ensman, Jr.
Rochester, New York

Don Farrant
St. Simons Island, Georgia

Warren Greshes
Speaking Of Success
New York, New York

Phil Kline
Diamondale, Michigan

Robert Populorum
Solutions Selling
   International
Wheaton, Illinois

Charles C. Schlom
Park Ridge, Illinois

CONTENTS

Topics include: Fear of the Unknown . . . Cold Calls
for Fun and Profit . . . The Slightly Warm Improvised
Sales Call Approach . . . The Challenge . . . First Get
Organized . . . Changing Habits . . . Analyze Time
Usage . . . Hints for Better Time Management . . . Planning
and Preparation . . . Travel and Waiting . . . Face-to-Face
Selling . . . Nonselling Activities . . . Quick Tips . . . What
Would You Do?

Topics include: Enthusiastic Customers Provide Leads . . .
Maintain Customer Contact . . . When Should You
Request a Referral? . . . Return the Favor . . . Quick
Tips . . . What Would You Do?

Topics include: Selling to Your Own Account List . . .
Back End First . . . Same Product — New Terms . . .
Add-Ons . . . Customized Offerings . . . Renew
Acquaintances . . . Sell to Former Customers . . . Selling
to "Like" Companies . . . Examples . . . Always Sell the
Easy Ones . . . On the Other Hand . . . Check Out
Financial Status . . . A Quick Guide to Uncovering Solid
Leads . . . Quick Tips . . . What Would You Do?

Introduction

Dear Sales Professional,

The old saying "Nothing worthwhile comes easily" certainly describes the work of obtaining new customers. No one would disagree that new accounts are not only worthwhile but also are really the lifeblood of any business.

Experienced salespeople know the task is difficult, but they also know that the work must be done, because every salesperson loses customers that must be replaced if sales objectives are to be met.

The ideas presented in this book, if used appropriately, will make you successful with new accounts. Every idea has been tested by active salespeople and proven valid.

It is easy to understand why some salespeople avoid prospecting and making that first call. Many have enough work with their regular customers to fill their days. This is business they can (usually) count on. Also, calling on regular accounts may be more enjoyable and less stressful.

What we must keep telling ourselves is that prospects spell opportunity that we will find nowhere else. We should also understand that the more we call on prospective customers, the more successful we'll become. The salesperson who achieves the best balance of old and new customers is the one who leads the pack.

The arithmetic is easy. How many accounts and how much dollar volume did you lose last year? How many new accounts and how much new dollar volume will you gain this year?

Getting new accounts may not have been easy for you in the past. After reading this book and applying the techniques described herein, it will get a whole lot easier.

In this convenient size, there's no reason you can't keep your copy of *More Than a Foot in the Door* in a handy location such as your desk or work area. We hope you'll pick it up frequently throughout the day to uncover a new tip or technique.

No matter how you use it, we hope you have as much fun reading *More Than a Foot in the Door* as we did producing it. Let us know what you think. Fax us in care of "The Professional Selling Series" at (312) 561-4842. We'd love to hear the sales tips that you've developed over the years so we can include them in a future edition!

— The Editors

HOW TO USE THE PROFESSIONAL SELLING SERIES

VOLUME 1: MORE THAN A FOOT IN THE DOOR

Topics covered: Tips for time management . . . How to get new accounts . . . Determining who your prospects should be . . . Qualifying prospects, including sizing up a corporation . . . Quick qualifier techniques . . . Making appointments, including getting in to see the "no-sees" . . . Improving telephone skills, including how to get past the gatekeepers . . . Overcoming first call jitters, including proven icebreakers.

VOLUME 2: CLOSE IT RIGHT, RIGHT NOW!

Topics covered: Understanding and preparing for the closing process . . . How to read your prospect . . . Overcoming buyer apprehension . . . Fear of closing . . . Little prods that help . . . Types of closes, including action, trial, inducement, and more . . . Steps to the close . . . Customized closes . . . When concessions are called for . . . Closing by phone . . . Managing the hesitation response and the last objection syndrome . . . Handling the bad-day buyer and the indecisive buyer . . . After the close, including add-ons, making the sale stick, and dealing with buyer remorse.

VOLUME 3: DO YOU HAVE ANY OBJECTIONS?

Topics covered: Objections under the microscope . . . Analyzing objections . . . Why you should welcome objections . . . Listening and asking questions . . . Proven objection-managing techniques . . . The price/quality issue . . . Building value into your products and services.

Though the topics covered in each volume are different, you will find that each has:

- *Practical tips* and *suggestions* . . . hands-on techniques practiced by highly successful sales professionals;

- *Stories* and *anecdotes* from sales luminaries to help you plan your approach and close the sale; and

- Dozens of *Quick Tips* that you can put into action immediately.

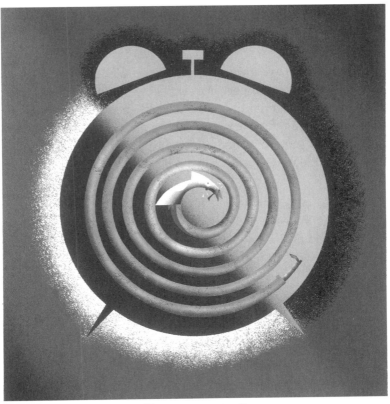

CHAPTER 1

IF ONLY I HAD TIME

Obtaining new customers is the lifeblood of any business. Yet in survey after survey, salespeople say that they'd like to do more prospecting, but they simply don't have enough time.

"I have to service existing customers, and that takes just about all of my time," is the hue and cry of many. While there is certainly truth in this statement for many salespeople, it still doesn't answer the key question, "How can I build my business without new accounts?"

A key fact hidden in all this discussion is simply that for most salespeople, it's easier to call on established accounts. There is no question that cold call reluctance has something to do with it.

Salespeople have a weekly or monthly sales quota to meet. If they call on a new prospect, they probably will come away without an immediate order, but have made progress that may result in an order next week or next month. On the other hand, they can spend a little more time and effort with an established customer and get a little more business immediately to meet the upcoming quota.

The old customer is right there. You don't have to find him, fight to get to see him, or figure out how to get his attention. You've got to find a new prospect, and catch her first before you can make progress with her.

Fear of the Unknown

Many salespeople shy away from prospecting because they fear the unknown. We all like to call on friendly customers. First call prospects may not want to see us, and if they do, they may not buy. Either way, we feel rejected.

Sometimes we become so fearful we don't even want to talk to receptionists or make phone inquiries.

More turn downs make us more depressed. What should we do?

Consider that the opposite is also true. The more success we have, the more encouraged we become. After the ice is broken we discover that the experience isn't so bad after all! Many salespeople worry needlessly about cold calls. The secret is simply to refuse to be discouraged. Once you hit pay dirt, you'll have a string of successes.

Keep in mind that only about one in 10 salespeople make regular prospecting calls. This means that many buyers are seldom approached by a salesperson who does not do business with them already. Think of the opportunity!

Rationalization and blaming the prospect is an easy path to take when making excuses for not making that first call, or for not going back a second time. You can blame your competitor for getting there first, for slashing prices or making concessions. You can say the buyer is too stupid to recognize your superior products or services.

This attitude is self-defeating. Face up to the possibility that the turn downs may be due, at least in part, to your own lack of skill in handling the prospect. Identify the problems, then fix them. This requires self-discipline and continuing efforts. In other words, a lot of looking in the mirror.

Cold Calls for Fun and Profit

Are cold calls a waste of time or are they a productive use of sales time? This is really a time and territory management question. Consider this familiar scenario:

Your salesperson drives 30 miles in urban rush hour traffic, leaving your office at 8:30 a.m. and arriving at the prospect's office at 9:40 a.m. A stop at the coffee shop to go over the proposal one last time, a last minute check in the mirror, and the salesperson is at the prospect's office at 9:55 a.m., five minutes early for the 10:00 a.m. appointment.

The call is a moderate success, a smaller order than hoped for was placed, but an order nonetheless. At 11:05 a.m. your salesperson calls the office to check messages, and phones a prospect to firm up an appointment later in the week. Thirty minutes later your sales rep is near the office of the next appointment, scheduled for 1:15 p.m. The salesperson then stops for lunch at a fast-food restaurant to review notes for the next call.

Finished with the appointment by 2:30 p.m., the sales rep drives to the last call of the day scheduled at 3:30 p.m. and is back at the office at 5 o'clock. After checking messages and finishing call reports, the salesperson is on the way home at 5:45 p.m. Quite a full day—or was it?

Could you have gotten more productive sales work from your rep in the area near that first call after one hour and 10 minutes of travel time during rush hour? Are cold calls just busy work, putting the salesperson in a bind for time to get to the next appointment and consequently lowering face-to-face sales performance? Or can cold calls increase productive face-to-face sales time, increase salespersons' prospect lists, while adding accounts and increasing volume?

The business buyer's tolerance for cold calls has deteriorated in recent years partly as the result of sloppy, unprepared, and unprofessional cold calls in the past. Bring up the subject of cold calls at any gathering of salespeople or sales managers and you'll be faced with a controversy. The supporters of cold calls are almost always a small minority. With a relatively negative response to cold calls, today's sales force needs to revise its approach to cold calling.

The Slightly Warm Improvised Sales Call Approach

This method of cold calling produces new prospects and literally doubles your selling time. Sales trainer and business writer Hal Fahner recalls being taught this method by Brent Wasik, a fellow rookie salesman in Detroit, a very long time ago. This approach is just as productive today, however:

"It calls for extra effort, hustle, constant thought and alert observation.

"Brent Wasik was never completely still. He moved constantly. He would have a phone at each ear. He had two briefcases, not just one. The second was packed for tomorrow's calls. Know the type? This method works more easily if the salesperson has the energy level that Brent displayed.

"Remember that *time and territory management* is the real subject. The modified cold call approach is a way of increasing productive face-to-face sales time.

"Set up the three-call appointment day the way it was described earlier. Modify that procedure as follows:

- Subdivide your sales territories into zones. Keep appointments on any single day within one zone. Eliminate long drives as much as possible.

- Use a cross-reference directory to see which companies are located near your appointment.

- Try not to travel during the rush hour. Start earlier and arrive well in advance of the scheduled appointment time. Use this time to do a little investigative research at the prospect company by talking to guards, secretaries, and dock workers. Find out what products and suppliers they use. This information may give you an edge in making a first call on the correct decision maker.

- If you find a prospect company on the spot that you missed in the cross-reference directory, have coffee at the restaurant across the street and discreetly question the waitress. You may even meet employees arriving early to have breakfast.

- At the end of a scheduled call, ask a few questions about neighboring businesses. The prospect may provide useful information for future calls.

- If no lunch appointment is scheduled, use that time to investigate the area.

- At the end of the day, if the last scheduled call concludes between 3:30 and 4:00 in the afternoon, spend an hour or so in the prospecting activities listed above.

- In small- and medium-size towns particularly, the Chamber of Commerce can sometimes be most helpful with information on local companies. Be discreet; that nice receptionist may be a relative of the president of the company you're checking on.

Organize ahead of time with a "slightly warm improvised" sales call in mind. Do the extra spade work beforehand and on the spot to prospect, qualify and gather information. This method will enable you to make appointments with the correct decision makers, showing them what your company has to offer in connection with what their company needs."

However, most salespeople can budget their time to go after new accounts if they really want to. Here are some ways that it can be accomplished.

THE CHALLENGE

First of all, you must start thinking of time management not as a problem but as an opportunity to get more accomplished in the same or less time than it now takes. The challenge is to free up time to do those things that your present schedule will not allow, assuming you are a pretty busy person already.

Many workers perform the same repetitive task over and over again, usually at a specified time and speed. A secretary does the work as it's given to him or her. The same is true for most other "white collar" jobs. But not a salesperson. In sales, there are choices. Of course, there are some constraints: Orders must be received from regular accounts, and a certain amount of paperwork must be done. But think of the choices, especially when it comes to prospecting, or the day or time to call on an account. You are in control much of the time. You can decide:

- Your route each day
- How long to spend on a call

- When to start work in the morning
- When to end your workday
- How you will make a presentation.

Because you have choices, you have many opportunities to make better use of your time and to manage your territory in such a way that more prospecting calls can be made.

Set a realistic quota of new calls per week. Realize that it will take a certain number of calls to produce an order, and that the new call demand must line up with your ideal balance between existing clients and new prospect calls.

You may not be able to do anything about the price of the products you sell or the service provided by the factory. So why not concentrate on those things that you can do something about—how you use your time and manage your territory.

The challenge is to find the best prospects and talk with the largest possible number of them.

That's the best-kept secret in the selling profession today. In the first instance, you must find the time to locate the best prospects. Depending on what you are selling, the "best" prospects could mean those who will purchase the largest quantities and/or the most profitable items, or it could mean those prospects *most likely* to purchase from you. After you have located the best prospects, then you must find the time to talk with them, to persuade them to buy from you.

Of course, you must be able to sell your products or services when you are in front of the prospect or customer. Some salespeople are better at this than others. But the critical difference is *the number of times* per day or week that you are able to make your presentation to good-quality prospects — those individuals who have both the authority and the ability to say "yes" to your proposal. It's as simple as that.

The challenge is to *do something* now to free up some of your time each day without affecting the quality or quantity of your present work. This is the first step.

Take one step at a time. Free up time to do one thing you have been wanting to do for a long time, and make this your reward. For example, you may want to spend 30 minutes or an hour cleaning out the trunk of your car, rearranging your briefcase, or getting your samples and advertising material straightened out. To prove to yourself that you can do a better job of managing your time, figure out a way to save that hour tomorrow by making better use of your time throughout the day.

Don't try to make big changes in your routine. It's too difficult and can become discouraging. Make little changes. Remember, the real payoff comes when one of your new time-saving ideas becomes a part of you and your daily routine. Think about it. If you do it every day, you get a *payoff* every day.

FIRST GET ORGANIZED

A self-organized salesperson is always in command of his or her time, never allowing outside forces to take over. This doesn't mean you should ignore others. It only means that you are "on top of things" because you have chosen to be directed from within. You are so well organized that interruptions must find a way to fit themselves into *your* schedule.

Being organized feels good. You know where you want to go, you know how you're going to get there, and then you set out on the journey, confident of success.

The reason for good self-organization is that the degree of success you will have with any single idea depends to a great extent on how well you are organized in your work. The entire process is a dynamic one. You start by being well organized, you try new time-saving techniques that work, and as a result you become even better organized!

How do you know when you have good self-organization? Here are six important ways to tell:

1. I am self-organized when I am in control of my time.

2. I am self-organized when I can explain where I will go, whom I will see, and what I will accomplish for a reasonable length of time in the future.

3. I am self-organized when I can handle unplanned work without it either affecting my overall performance or putting me permanently behind.

4. I am self-organized when I know in advance how I will handle an emergency or interruption.

5. I am self-organized when I know how to successfully get others to help me get my work done — and then successfully do it.

6. I am self-organized when I have a system to handle any routine or repetitive task, thereby eliminating the need to give it "thinking time" at each occurrence.

CHANGING HABITS

If you are going to practice self-organization, you will need to break some old habits and replace them with new ones. We all know that this is not easy. Sometimes we wish we didn't have so many habits. Wouldn't it be nice to do things completely different each day? Not really. It might be nice to do a *few things* differently, but changing your entire routine would be most uncomfortable.

The key is to change one habit at a time, and replace that habit with a new one.

For example, try a new route that will reduce driving time. Start 15 minutes earlier each day. Skip the afternoon coffee break. Get one order each day by phone rather than making a personal visit. This will free up time for one or two prospecting calls each day.

ANALYZE TIME USAGE

A good way to start making time for prospecting work is to analyze how you now use your time. Keep a time log every day for one or two weeks. Record, in 30-minute increments, what you do each day. Then analyze it to see where time can be saved. You'll be surprised at the number of time-saving opportunities.

Look at your current call pattern to see if improvements can be made. Review your call reports for the last several months to see what you can learn. Warning signs include too much time with low-volume accounts, too much time driving, overservicing some accounts, and spending too much time with friendly customers.

After a thorough analysis, ask yourself these questions:

1. What routine activities can I eliminate, reduce, or delegate to others?

2. How much time will this save? Hours per day, per week?

3. How can I become better organized? Be specific.

4. What specific changes will I make and when will I make them?

5. Specifically, how much time each day/week will I spend searching for new business?

HINTS FOR BETTER TIME MANAGEMENT

The salesperson's job falls more or less into four areas, as far as time usage is concerned:

- Planning and preparation
- Travel and waiting
- Face-to-face selling
- Nonselling activities.

Here are some useful, field-tested ideas to improve your time management in each area.

Planning and preparation

1. Determine call frequency by volume or profit potential rather than by convenience of making the call.

2. Know exactly where you are going each week and each day. Write it down.

3. Schedule your calls as far in advance as possible — never less than one week.

4. Eliminate all calls that have very low return.

5. Use the telephone for calls that need not be made in person.

6. Keep adequate records on each account and review them before making the call.

7. Have samples and presentation materials ready *before* the call.

8. Determine the best time to see the decision maker and schedule for that time, if possible.

9. Always have back-up calls close to your important calls.

10. Check your car each morning to see that you have all necessary samples and materials for the day.

Travel and waiting

1. Reduce travel time by developing good routing practices.

2. Make appointments with key accounts, while still allowing for some changes in your schedule each day.

3. Don't skip around. Lay out a route and stick to it.

4. Plan meals and travel at times when buyers are not available.

5. Use waiting time for record keeping, making appointments, and planning the next day's work.

6. If you have a long wait, make another call close by, then return.

7. Avoid emergency calls. Suggest that you will stop by when you are next in the area.

Face-to-face sellling

1. See the person who can say "yes."

2. Plan each call in advance. Know what you want and then ask for it.

3. Get to the point quickly; minimize small talk.

4. Send advance information when possible.

5. Listen, take notes, qualify, and give thought to what you should say before making the presentation.

6. Sell the full line whenever possible. Make the largest sale you can on each call.

7. Have everything you need with you, to avoid going back to the car.

8. Before you leave, make an appointment for the next visit.

Nonselling activities

1. Delegate, if possible. Get others to help you, including customer service personnel.

2. Stay away from the office, especially on Monday mornings and Friday afternoons.

3. Complete paperwork before or after the best selling hours.

4. Watch coffee breaks, long lunches, and late starts.

5. Don't conduct personal business during your best selling hours.

6. Avoid the urge to goof off after a big sale or a string of bad luck.

7. Learn how to say "no" and resist any work that takes away from your selling time.

8. Avoid nonessential service to customers.

QUICK TIPS

- Prepare a weekly and daily call schedule.

- Use a "to-do" list every day.

- Take advantage of your high- and low-energy periods. Plan your toughest sales calls during high-energy times and your routine tasks during low-energy times.

- Don't avoid the long or difficult tasks because you can't find one large block of time to complete them. Instead, keep chipping away, breaking them down into smaller units.

- Make quick decisions on details and unimportant matters.

- Give every job a due date and get it done by that date.

- Worrying, pondering, or doing busy work while delaying decisions or important tasks won't get the job done. Getting started is the key.

- Group similar tasks together, such as making a number of phone calls during one time period.

- When not working, try to relax. Total relaxation for short periods of time renews your energy and makes you feel better.

- Be of good cheer! It's contagious. Others will treat you better and you'll feel better as a result.

WHAT WOULD YOU DO?

I would like to do more new-account selling, but, honestly, I get so many interruptions every day — customers calling, office calling, etc. — that I run out of time.

Do you have any advice about avoiding these time-consuming interruptions?

Sometimes interruptions can't be avoided — an important, unexpected phone call comes through, or a crisis erupts concerning your largest customer. Those are examples of interruptions that you must simply learn to accept.

In addition to unavoidable interruptions, however, there are many other kinds that can be avoided. Practice the following protections to ward off avoidable interruptions:

Plan in advance. Schedule specific times during the day to meet with others and make and accept phone calls. Inform others of your practice and abide by your rules.

Put a sign on your door. A "Do Not Disturb" sign on your door will ward off interruptions. Make sure you inform others when you will again be available and remember to take the sign down.

Set limits. If you find short meetings are turning into long ones, set time limits. Inform others at the onset that you have a limited amount of time. Stick to the limits you set!

Meet elsewhere. It is much easier to leave a meeting that is taking place outside your office than to leave one taking place inside.

Don't invite others. Having an office with several empty chairs or comfortable couches invites others to "drop in." Remove any extra furniture from your office to reduce these temptations.

Face your chair away from the door. If your chair is facing away from the door, you won't make eye contact with others, inviting them to stop in.

Another positive aspect of this arrangement of furniture is that it is less distracting; you won't be tempted to watch others pass.

You can say "no." If someone asks if you have a free minute, say "no" (if it would be an interruption). Suggest a better time, such as during your designated meeting time.

In addition to avoiding interruptions, here are some other things you can do.

- Get an early start each day
- Preplan the day's activities
- Make and confirm all your sales appointments
- Use waiting time effectively
- Minimize coffee breaks
- Handle paperwork promptly
- Qualify your prospects
- Set goals
- Keep a time log
- Evaluate your use of time.

SUMMARY

Before you complain that you don't have enough time to go after new business, stop and consider what's at stake. You and every other salesperson lose accounts, many times through no fault of your own — customers go out of business, product lines change — there are many reasons. This means that you must constantly get new customers to take the place of those you lose.

Also ask yourself if part of the problem is cold call reluctance. If so, think about all the times that you get really tired of the same customers talking about the same things and calls whose outcomes are highly predictable.

Think about the fun and excitement of meeting new people and at the same time being able to put your many selling skills to the test.

Prospecting for new customers can be an adventure as well as a sure way to dramatically increase your sales and the financial and other rewards that come with it.

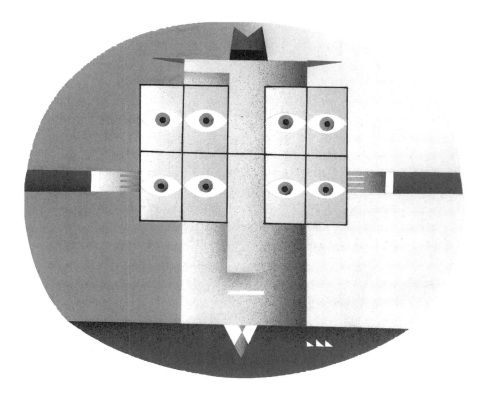

CHAPTER 2

HOW TO ASK FOR AND RECEIVE MORE REFERRALS

Referrals are the lifeblood of selling. They increase your chances of succeeding and add value to each prospecting call.

Like every salesperson in the world, you would far rather call on a referred prospect than make a cold call. The odds of obtaining a face-to-face appointment are infinitely better from a referral. Yet most salespeople never seem to generate enough of them. Here is a four-step process to help obtain a greater number of referrals and ultimately increase sales.

1. Ask! The single biggest reason salespeople do not generate referrals is that they don't ask for them.

Your satisfied customers can be tremendous allies for you. They are gold mines of qualified leads. And those leads are just sitting there for the asking.

Greet your established customers with this statement: *"I have a problem and I need your help."* People nearly always respond favorably to such a request, because we all feel flattered when asked for help. Then you can say, "You bought this product and are happy with it. I want to be of the same service to others as I have been to you. Whom do you know that might enjoy owning this product?"

Your satisfied customers know what problems their friends have, what they are currently looking for, what their needs are. So just ask. Ask every time.

Get all the information you can from your satisfied customers, and then ask for some advice. Ask whom you should call first, what his or her most pressing need is, what the person is looking for. Ask for some coaching — what you should do and how you should do it. Most people love the idea of becoming a coach.

You can even go one step further. Ask your satisfied customer to introduce you. This gives you credibility you can't get any other way. This is the ultimate endorsement — having people without a vested interest in the outcome declare what a wonderful product they have discovered and how much they respect you. Ask for a referral, ask for an introduction, ask them to make a phone call. Just ask!

Another way to network for prospects is by asking "centers of influence." These are friendly contacts who know you and want to help you. The list might include relatives, neighbors, old friends, and professional acquaintances. Approach them with the same kind of introductory statement you use with customers. A valuable center of influence can, over time, refer many solid names to your prospect inventory.

Someone who knows many people and/or has strong business ties is the best source for leads. Pass out your business cards wherever you go. Many people have wide circles of friends, and if the need for your product or service comes up in a conversation it just might be mentioned that "I know someone who sells that!"

You meet a few people each week who are potential prospects, or know someone who is a good prospect for your product or service. Perhaps you don't talk about your job because you feel it is presumptuous to do so.

You don't have to give everyone you meet a sales pitch, but it is a good idea to tell them who you are, who you work for, and what you sell.

Other potentially rich referral sources are the vendors and merchants with whom you spend money. They will respond to your request for help because they appreciate *your* business.

You can also swap referrals with noncompeting businesses. Such cooperative trading can result in names you might have overlooked or been unaware of.

This works very well when you're traveling overnight and staying at a hotel or motel. You get to meet other salespeople who are also interested in getting leads. Sharing information with these individuals can be both a pleasant and rewarding use of your free time.

In each of these categories, you are making use of a disciplined acquaintanceship — people sharing ideas and information through personal contacts.

2. Ask for a specific number of referrals. By asking for a specific number, you're framing the question and making it easier for the person to answer. If I asked you to name everyone you know, could you? On the other hand, if I said, "Name your three closest friends," not only could you do that, but it would be easy. Remember, if you make it easy for people to act, they will.

3. Use a referral sheet. You don't need anything fancy, just a lined sheet of paper with five columns across the top (Name, Company Name, Title, Address, Phone Number) and numbers running down the left side. These numbers should only go up to the number of referrals you want.

When asking for referrals, always have this sheet out in front of the person you're asking. It shows you're serious, and when he or she hears you ask while simultaneously staring at that empty referral sheet, that person is receiving a nonverbal message that says, "Fill 'er up." Get all the names first, then ask for details of addresses and phone numbers. This way, if you are interrupted, you still walk away with several names rather than one name and all the information about that one person.

If Mr. Jones refers you to Ms. Black, ask him a little about her. Ask: "What do you like about her?"

Let's say Mr. Jones says, "She's a high-energy manager who turned her department around when nobody else could."

You might then ask: "Do you think I can help her do an even better job?" and "Do you think she would meet with me?"

If Mr. Jones answers "yes" to both questions, call Ms. Black and tell her that you've talked with Mr. Jones, who described her as a high-energy manager who turned around her department when nobody else could.

Ms. Black will likely be charmed by this remark and thank you for the compliment. Now tell her that Mr. Jones also thought that she might benefit from a meeting with you, and ask for a brief appointment. You'll probably get a go-ahead — because Ms. Black will view you not as a "cold-calling salesperson," but as a "promising new acquaintance."

4. Ask the kinds of questions that can be answered. Even when they bother to ask for referrals, many salespeople ask the wrong way. They might say, "You wouldn't happen to know anybody who would be interested in buying anything, would you?" Aside from being too open-ended, this question begs for a negative response.

Figure out what markets you need to be in and what kinds of individuals you want to sell to. Most people know and associate with others exactly like themselves. People at the vice-president level know other vice presidents. Business owners know other business owners. If you were working the small-business market, you might ask an owner, "Could you give me the names of three other business owners you are friendly with?" Or, to a vice president in a large organization, "Could you give me the names of three other people at your level I might be able to talk to?" Let's face it — if you wanted to sell to high–net-worth individuals, would you prospect on the unemployment line?

ENTHUSIATIC CUSTOMERS PROVIDES LEADS

Ask a satisfied customer how he likes a certain salesperson and he's apt to say something like, "Oh, he's okay. I get what I pay for. But the enthusiastic customer jumps at the chance to brag about his salesperson. "She's the greatest! Let me tell you what she did for me just last month." If you deliver what the customer wants at a fair price, without any problems, he's satisfied. But it takes more than that to retain customers and increase sales.

What's the key to making customers enthusiastic? How do you keep them from going to competitors? Deliver more than customers expect, knowing this breeds enthusiasm. Enthusiasm produces a climate that ensures loyalty of the customer and increased sales.

Here are some suggestions the professionals have for producing and maintaining enthusiastic customers. Try the ones that best fit your selling situation.

- **Keep in touch.** Check after delivery to see that things are going well. Check again later and ask for leads on new prospects. Write a thank-you letter or make a telephone call.

- **Handle complaints promptly.** Problems are inevitable. Don't ignore them. They grow with neglect. Do more than the customer expects in satisfying the complaint.

- **Be a friend.** Think of the customer as a friend and do things for him or her accordingly. Send birthday cards. Send a postcard while you're on vacation.

- **Give praise when it's due.** Look for things for which you can give legitimate praise: awards, increased earnings, a big order. Congratulate the customer personally for awards, election to an office or honors. Customers appreciate attention, too.

- **Send prospects to your customers.** If your customer is in business, send leads or refer prospects to him or her. It's human nature to respond in kind to anyone who does us a favor.

- **Ask for prospect leads.** How does this increase the customer's enthusiasm for you? We're always flattered when asked for help, suggesting we're important.

There is a maxim in selling that goes, "Business goes where it's invited and stays where it is well treated." Take time to treat your customers as you would like to be treated, and you'll change them from just so-so satisfied customers to enthusiastic sales-getters.

MAINTAIN CUSTOMER CONTACT

Want a steady stream of referrals? You can generate word-of-mouth advertising by encouraging it. Stay in regular contact with your customers. Ask how service has been, and take action to improve it if necessary.

Find out what old problems have been solved and get facts and figures to use in presentations to prospects. Also, discover what future plans your customers have and share data your company has (or could obtain) on the subject.

Don't forget to mention your internal and external support network whenever a contact of yours could assist a customer. You're setting an example you hope they'll follow.

Ask your satisfied customers to tell their colleagues about the results your products or services helped them achieve. Supply them with an extra brochure or fact sheet to facilitate this.

Another tip: Make sure that your best and most satisfied customers have several of your business cards on hand to pass out when they recommend you.

One successful salesperson we know always gives new prospects three of her business cards at a first meeting. Is this overkill? No — she says customers appreciate having multiple cards in case they misplace one or would like one for their Rolodex and another for their wallet or card file. (And this gives them one to give away, too.)

WHEN SHOULD YOU REQUEST A REFERRAL?

The best time to ask is after delivery of the product or service. You have given the customer something, so he or she is feeling good and will be in a good frame of mind to give you something. It's not a good idea to ask for referrals upon closing a sale. You're asking for too much at once.

Another good time to ask for referrals is when you've been turned down on a sales call. First, you have nothing to lose. You can't be any deader than dead. Second, most people feel bad about saying "no" and would love to say "yes" to something, especially since it won't cost anything.

RETURN THE FAVOR

Remember that referrals from your customers are favors — and favors should be returned.

In other words, don't just *take* referrals; *give* them back. Appreciative customers will respond with more referrals — and more business.

Put customers who need products that other customers sell in touch with each other by:

• *Supplying leads.* Pass along industry knowledge to your customers. Suggest specific companies that might need a particular product. If possible, provide a contact name.

• *Making introductions.* Ask customers: "Is there a company you've been trying to get into, but can't?" Then, make a few phone calls and pave the way.

You might also consider offering a "bonus" for referring new customers. Depending on the product you sell, the bonus might be in the form of cash back, a small gift, or a discount.

Above all, thank your referral sources and report back to them the results of the referred calls.

QUICK TIPS

- Start with your most satisfied customers. Offer a compliment, then ask for referrals.

- Customers who are well known and highly successful make the best references. Do you have customers who are:

  — leaders in the community?
  — leaders in their business or industry?
  — financially successful?
  — often in the news?

  Mention them to prospective customers.

- Referral sources need not be customers. If your neighbor knows a prospect, use the name to help you get an appointment. This "endless chain" approach is a way of saying indirectly to a prospect, "Check me out with someone you know."

- Make it a point to ask your customers about their participation in professional, business, and social organizations — everything from the Chamber of Commerce to the Lions Club to the country club. The "joiners" are your best referral sources.

WHAT WOULD YOU DO?

Over time, I've developed a very professional relationship with my clients. To ask for referrals seems to me to cheapen these relationships by placing some kind of monetary value on them. I need referrals but don't think it's a good idea to ask my clients. What should I do?

Because you've known your clients for some time, I'm sure you've developed personal as well as professional relationships. Obviously, they like you and your organization or they wouldn't continue to buy from you.

Just because you sell professional products to professional people doesn't mean that they view your relationship the same way.

I know you will be pleasantly surprised when you ask for referrals. Because of your concern, you might start by saying to one of your clients, "I want to ask how you would feel if I asked for one or two referrals." Explain that others in your company have found this approach effective and you would like to try it.

Don't be concerned if one or two clients turn you down, because not everyone is so inclined.

If you follow the suggestions outlined in this chapter, you will be highly successful both in obtaining referrals and gaining new clients as a result.

SUMMARY

Getting referrals is the key to successful selling. If you ask for them every time you make a sale, you should never have to make another cold call. People want to help. You've done them a favor by satisfying their need, and you've established mutual trust. What better time to ask for a referral than when they are happiest with their decision and before any problems or complaints have had an opportunity to arise?

Be specific when you ask for referrals. Suggest categories of related businesses, suppliers, or membership associations that may be interested in your product or service. Ask the person for five names and write each down on a separate index card to be placed later in your prospect file. Before leaving, thank the client for helping you. A simple question like "If you were in my position, whom would you call on first?" can give important hints on timing and readiness and confirm your commitment to follow through on the client's recommendations.

If the people named were there, your client would introduce you to them. Suggesting this, ask the client if he or she would mind making a telephone introduction.

After the sale, there are also good times to gather referrals such as when you are delivering your product personally or making a follow-up call on that account. People want to help. Let them.

CHAPTER 3

DETERMINE WHO YOUR
PROSPECTS SHOULD BE

There are nearly as many theories regarding prospects as there are styles of selling. There are, however, some suggestions that are universally accepted. These include:

- Selling more product or a different product line to your current customers

- Selling to customers who have done business with your company in the past but no longer do

- Selling to businesses like those on your current customer list.

SELLING TO YOUR OWN ACCOUNT LIST

Every salesperson knows that he or she is not getting 100 percent of the potential from most customers. They do buy from other sources! The critical questions you should ask yourself about any account are:

1. What percentage of their total usage am I getting?

2. What are my chances of getting additional volume?

The answer to the first question will help you determine the additional sales volume that it's possible to get. The answer to the second question, though more difficult to determine, will help you decide how much time you should be willing to spend in order to try to get this extra business.

You probably have more than one product or service to offer for sale; in fact, you probably have many items to offer. And, chances are, many of these items are not promoted and sold — because some products or services are easier to sell, pay a larger commission percentage, or encounter less intense competition than others.

Salespeople tend to work hardest on the products or services that they feel the most comfortable with — and, as a result, neglect other excellent opportunities for new sales of other products and services within their own accounts.

The fact that your customers purchase something from you proves that they trust you and your company. Take advantage of this! Half of the work of making any new sale involves convincing the buyer that you and your company are trustworthy and capable of providing a viable product and top-notch service.

You've already proven that you can do this with the products you currently provide. Any new sale you approach in these accounts will be infinitely easier to close than with a new account who has never heard of you or your company.

You need only identify the correct product or service to meet the customer's needs. Then offer to consolidate billing for these items.

To sell your existing customers new offerings from your company, take these steps:

1. Identify several product lines or services that you have previously not spent much time with, and do some research on them.

2. Ask your sales manager for information concerning each account. Then ask your colleagues, members of your company's marketing department, and others in your company for any information or advice about the new offerings you've targeted.

3. Use the good relationships with your current accounts to pursue new sales. Because the buyers know you and your company, your knowledge of products or services will be enough to allow you to pursue the business. Remember: Your status as an expert can go a long way toward tallying new sales.

Also, established customers have payment records we know and accept.

BACK END FIRST

The notion of contacting existing customers is "back-end" marketing—the back end is contacting people after they have purchased. But, this type of marketing is what you should be doing first, before embarking on a less focused and more expensive "front end" (attempting to generate new customers).

Although profit opportunities abound in current customers, let's look at three potential revenue sources: 1) same product/service, new terms; 2) add-on complementary product/service; and 3) customized product/service.

Same product — new terms

One-time customers who are satisfied with your product or service may not, without some prompting, automatically reorder the same product. Take, for example, a service that is sold on a one-time basis, whether it is a home extermination service, or a professional business consultation service.

Salespeople who recognize the value of prior customers will offer: long-term contracts at a reduced rate; discounts for repeat purchases; and quantity incentive offers' benefits for referring customers.

It is surprising how many sales reps don't contact customers unless the reps need something. Simply contacting them often results in sales. After all, these people know the product/service, they have bought before and are satisfied—a relatively easy sell. Going beyond just contact, offering new terms and a choice of terms serve as an incentive to the customers to do more business with you. New terms are only part of back-end marketing.

Add-ons

There is almost no product or service that cannot be supplemented with a follow-up or "add-on" product. For example, a computer training company offered an easy-to-create resume program and later a program that generates business cards and letterhead. Both products were offered to their original customers, and a significant percentage bought the new offerings.

It's not necessary to wait until after a sale to contact your customers. Include offers in every package, invoice, or product instruction book, documentation, or any literature. By offering your customers a related product, you give them the opportunity to reinforce their original purchase. They are ready to buy, they want to buy. Don't disappoint them.

Ask auto dealers about their success with add-on products. Many make more profit on the accessories customers decide to buy after they have made their initial purchase than they did on their original sale.

Add-on sales are not limited to a one-time, add-on accessory or product enhancement. In fact, they can be endless. Completely new products aren't necessary. A good example is in the computer software industry. As soon as you are comfortable with one version of software, the company offers a "new, improved" update.

Similarly, once you have read a book on a profitable technique, you can often learn more by purchasing the cassette learning services, with updates, specialized applications, and so on.

Keep your products or services in front of the customer. They need your updates, add-ons, new methods, improvements—all of it. Don't make them search for you. Many won't.

Customized offerings

Although not as common as add-ons, companies worldwide are making customized products and services available to their current customers. A simple example is offering the same merchandise in different packaging, so it's more convenient for the customer: a travel pack or an economy size. How many different sizes and shapes of aspirin containers can you find? Everything from a two-tablet pack to a large jar containing thousands—some are even waterproof.

If you supply products to resellers, contact them to see what variations in size, quantity, packaging, and other custom features they could have used to meet their customers' needs. Maybe they already have a wish list and are looking for vendors who can meet their customers' requests.

How do you customize a service? Some service companies already offer a customized version of their services and don't market it that way. Anytime the service is modified or made unique, it is a customized one. For example, in training seminars, the case studies are based on the clients' specific products and the customers they deal with. If company employees have been trained in the principles and techniques necessary for them to function effectively, it only makes sense to follow up with product-specific or customer-specific training.

Look what the delivery services have done to mold their product (delivering packages) offerings to meet customers' exacting requirements. You have your choice of overnight morning delivery, economy two-day guaranteed, two day only for certain metropolitan areas, speedy international delivery, under two pounds economy, overnight letter only, and more. An endless list, and still changing. One of the services has a newsletter-like flyer which gives tips on overseas deliveries, customs requirements, and even unique aspects of local culture in selected international markets. They haven't forgotten the customer's business and want to keep him or her informed on current services which can be shaped to match their desires.

RENEW ACQUAINTANCES

These three profit opportunities—new terms, add-ons and customized products—are just a few of those available from your highest-probability buyers who have been loyal and supportive in the past—your customers. In today's climate of scarce resources, there is no need to funnel them all toward the elusive (albeit attractive to the uninitiated) new customer. Save time, and money, while rapidly building your sales by targeting your existing customers.

SELLING TO FORMER CUSTOMERS

One term for them is "orphans." These are the customers your company sold to in the past but with whom it has lost contact. They are the ones who may have been lost to a competitor, or they may be the customers who were called on by the salesperson who left the company.

Orphans have several things in common: They have purchased the types of products you sell and they can afford them, but they are no longer buying from your company.

Your company's files, customer lists, old proposals, and old orders all contain a great deal of information about these orphans. These records already indicate who the buying influences are, who decides on the technical specifications, and who decides how much money can be spent — and when. Above all, these records indicate what types of products these former customers used. This is information that would take you many sales calls and a lot of time and money to determine.

Bear in mind that some of these people may have left the orphaned company. The specific event that caused your company to lose the business could well be a thing of the past. What exists today is a bright future with opportunities to get new business. You are going to start fresh, but with an advantage you could only dream of — the historical details and background, which normally take years to acquire.

So dig into those files, get the information, and make a prospect list using your competitive advantage as a guide.

Then get on the phone, give them a call, or make a personal sales call to verify and update the information.

Remember, you're the new kid on the block, so you won't be held accountable for the mistakes of the past. There's only one direction to go — up to new sales.

You now have a fully qualified prospect with one-tenth of the effort. Now all you have to do is determine current needs and desires and start selling. And you can sell with confidence because of the information you have previously gathered.

SELLING TO "LIKE" COMPANIES

Most salespeople have only 2,080 selling hours in the entire year — and some of that time is spent traveling.

Likewise, most buyers have only 2,080 buying hours in the whole year. Therefore, those prospects allot some of that precious time only to those salespeople who can show that they can help with the buying process.

By applying the concept of "selective prospecting," you can save both yourself and your prospects some of this precious time. Selective prospecting begins with a thorough knowledge of one's best customers. That knowledge is acquired by studying the ways customers apply your products. Why did your customers buy your product? What benefits are they now enjoying because of those purchases?

Once you have answers to these questions, consult manufacturers' directories for companies with the same Standard Industrial Classification (SIC) code. Look for the names of "suspects" who might become prospects. You should be able to locate many companies with the same type of operation as that of your existing customers in that industry. These suspects are now your "selected prospects." Call them for an appointment.

When a buyer receives a call from a stranger, he or she is

inclined to be evasive. But when that stranger quickly describes what he or she has done for others with similar needs, that same buyer is inclined to listen — and grant an interview.

Selective prospecting requires a lot of homework — everything from being conversant with the varied applications of your products and the benefits your customers are enjoying to knowing the functions of your existing customers so that you can find prospects with the same functions. But your telephone call for an appointment is made very easy because of this homework.

These three prospecting sources — current customers, former customers, and companies like your customers — are basic and readily understandable. The different approaches arise from the various ways of classifying the best of these prospects.

DETERMINE PROSPECTS' POTENTIAL VALUE

Because there are always more prospective customers out there than any salesperson can get to, you need some way to assess the potential value of the prospect to you. When you consider your chances of getting some new business, an important consideration is *how long* you think it will take you to get it, either in weeks, months, or number of calls. Either way, it costs you something.

A quick way to arrive at "potential value" is to multiply the amount of the business you expect to get by the chances you believe you have of getting it. This chance can be expressed as a percentage. For example, if you think there is one chance in four of getting a certain order, this can be expressed as 25 percent of the size of the potential order.

EXAMPLES

You think you have only one chance in four of getting the General Motors order, but if you do get it, it will be for $1 million:

$1,000,000 x .25 = $250,000 (potential value).

You think you have a fifty-fifty chance of getting the order from Ford Motor Company, which will be for $650,000:

$650,000 x .50 = $325,000 (potential value).

Which of these two customers would you see first? Ford Motor Company, right?

Many salespeople always go for the "sure thing" accounts. That's fine if the accounts can produce sizable volume and profit for you, but in many cases the "sure thing" accounts are so small that no significant volume is ever achieved, regardless of the salesperson's success rate. The problem with such an approach is that you never have time left to go after the big ones!

ALWAYS SELL THE EASY ONES

Some salespeople are favorites of the sales manager because of the desirable business they bring in. Others are always in trouble with the sales manager because of the *un*desirable business they bring in. There's a pattern here!

One of the most successful salespeople we know gave this insight into his success. "Sell the good ones, sell the big ones," he said. "Why? Because the good ones and the big ones have the money. They're smart. They know a good deal when they see one. You can *sell* to them."

He continued: "The small ones and the struggling ones can't buy. They want a special deal if they're interested at all. They're a pain. They take forever to sell. Then you spend months trying to straighten out the special deal you gave them, and they're never happy. They don't know a good deal when they see one. You'll never sell much to marginal accounts and you'll never make much money."

"The truth of the matter is that it takes just as much time and effort to sell a small one as to a big one. The big ones are those your sales manager would give anything to get. They have the money and the need. If you can solve their problem with your product, they see that quickly and buy. They don't ask for unreasonable concessions or special customizing or financing."

Marginal buyers are marginal because they don't have a clear need for your product. They demand product modifications, unreasonable financing arrangements, or even discounts, because they don't see the value your product gives them.

Likewise, what's true for one salesperson is not necessarily valid for another.

ON THE OTHER HAND

Many sales professionals feel like the rep quoted previously: "Sell the big ones; sell the easy ones." There's another side to this coin, however. Many a sales commission has been generated from sales to small companies.

If many of your competitors subscribe to the "think-big" philosophy of selling only to the big guys, this leaves vast numbers of smaller businesses neglected. Small accounts are attractive for several reasons:

- Small companies tend to show the most customer loyalty. Small companies really appreciate it when you take the time to work with them — especially when your competitors don't. You'll win their devoted loyalty by helping them refine work processes with your advanced knowledge or introducing them to new labor-saving products. Even if such customers enter a period in which your products aren't needed, they'll remember you later when their needs change.

- Small accounts are less expensive to maintain. Small companies tend not to expect the "wining, dining, and golfing" that large companies do. In addition, in small companies, there are usually not as many decision makers to accommodate.

- Small firms are relatively easy to deal with. There is usually a less formal, more personable style in the air at a small company. Enjoy it — and win friends as well as customers.

- Small accounts are less damaging to lose than large accounts. If you do happen to lose a small account or two, not a lot of harm is done. By contrast, if you lose a large account, you could suddenly be facing a major reduction in profits. In addition, you stand less chance of getting stuck with excess inventory from small accounts.

And keep in mind that a small company today might be a big company tomorrow. Some of the most successful companies of this decade started off in entrepreneurs' garages — and your help "back in the early days" will be remembered.

CHECK OUT FINANCIAL STATUS

Remember, no matter how good your prospects might look, they are ultimately only as good as they are financially secure. Investigate their financial standing, and, if the news is bad, use your time to pursue more financially sound prospects.

It's also in your long-term interest to think beyond the immediate sale. Give precedence to prospects who are in growth industries or who are likely to buy more than once.

A QUICK GUIDE TO UNCOVERING SOLID LEADS

One of the oldest controversies in sales is the one over "the best approach," meaning what is the most effective way of soliciting prospects ... cold calling in person, cold telephone calling, or direct mail? No one has ever resolved this issue to anyone else's satisfaction, except perhaps to agree that there is no one right approach.

The best approach varies by type of industry, competitors' activities, type of product sold, territory, personal style, and many other variables. It is virtually impossible to select the one best way to uncover solid leads.

It is possible, however, to discuss the relative merits and disadvantages of each approach. Here are just a few things to consider when trying to decide which combination of approaches to use:

	Advantages	**Disadvantages**
Cold calling in person	• Best way to discover customers new to the territory prior to their buying decision(s).	• Takes the most time. Many prospects resent the intrusion of a visit without an appointment.
	• Can complete all necessary paperwork and finalize sale on one contact.	
	• Best method of developing rapport quickly.	
	• Some prospects appreciate the difficulty in cold calling and react more positively.	

	Advantages	Disadvantages
Cold calling by phone	• Most time-effective method.	• More difficult to establish rapport over the phone. • Many customers feel as strongly about the intrusiveness of a phone call as they do about a sales rep stopping by without an appointment.
Mailings	• Psychologically, recipients feel more "in control" than when confronted with call or visit. Will often react more positively as a result.	• Cannot match mood of approach to prospects' personality. • Takes longer to get reaction from prospect. Consequently, it takes longer to make the sale.

Is your business almost completely reliant on a high volume of contacts? Does it require a quick sale? Is face-to-face rapport-building an important element of your sales process? Would direct mail duplicate the efforts of your marketing department? These are the kinds of questions to ask yourself while reviewing the comparison grid above to come up with the best approach for your company's sales contacts.

QUICK TIPS

- The world is full of prospects. In trying to find the best ones, ask yourself two questions:

    1. What will I have if I get it (sales, profit)?
    2. What will it cost to get it and keep it (time, money)?

    The answer to these two questions is sometimes difficult to obtain, but you have to try. Sometimes you'll get bad information. Sometimes you'll get little or no information. Sometimes you go with your hunches.

    But go ahead you must. That's better than calling down the street or in alphanumeric order. Or worse, ignoring them completely.

- Don't be afraid to ask a prospect the quantities they purchase and any other questions that will help you determine their potential. Most will tell you, so why guess? Customers understand that you must determine not only what items they might purchase, but also the quantities, before you can make a proper proposal or presentation.

- The customers and prospects you talk with know many other prospects for your products and services. Be sure not only to ask them for names, but also ask them to size up each prospect's potential. They'll help you sort the wheat from the chaff.

WHAT WOULD YOU DO?

I am one of seven who sell copiers, fax machines, and other office machines in a major metropolitan market. There are no assigned territories. Since almost every office needs at least some of the products I sell, how shall I determine where my best prospects are?

Talk with the other six salespeople for their suggestions. Then develop a preliminary strategy based on everything you've learned, plus your own experience and observations.

You may decide to work a specific geographic area that no one else covers. Or you might decide that you'll focus on the downtown area only.

Certainly you'll want to spend time with large users. Even so, many big companies buy only replacement products, so don't expect them to buy in quantity simply because you have an improved product.

As you are most likely aware, customers with heavy machine usage are better prospects because the equipment wears out faster.

You will find that certain types of users are easier to sell to than others. Concentrate on them and work referrals vigorously.

Eventually, through experience, you'll learn where the best prospects are located.

SUMMARY

Ask any experienced salesperson, "Who are your best prospects?" and you'll most likely hear, "Ones most like my biggest and best customers."

Ask this same salesperson then to name his or her top 20 prospects, and you may hear, "Well, I'll have to give that a little thought" or a similar remark.

On the other hand, the salesperson who really knows the best prospects would reach into his or her briefcase and hand you a list, with a record of calls made or planned. Now that's someone who knows where the gold is buried and has already started mining it!

For most salespeople, developing a list of prospects is not difficult. The real problem (and work) comes when trying to sort them out according to potential.

The problem is magnified when you consider the level of difficulty of obtaining the first order.

By forcing yourself to make a judgment on the *chances* of success with each prospect, then comparing those chances with the total dollar volume at stake, you will arrive at a more realistic potential for each. Some salespeople will spend inordinate amounts of time with a very large prospect, trying to obtain distribution or usage on a product or service where the chances of success are almost nil. While it is true that placement, when achieved, will produce high sales and profits for the salesperson and his or her company, the fact remains that chances for success are slim to nonexistent.

Your first step in determining potential is to obtain usage information. It does little good to drive past a store, factory, or office building and count the cars in the parking lot. You've got to get a lot more specific than that.

Finally, remember that new prospects appear regularly. Keep your eyes peeled for them, and get there ahead of your competitors.

CHAPTER 4

QUALIFYING THE PROSPECT

"What," asks author Stan Golomb, "is the purpose of being in business?"

If you answered, "To make a profit," he says you're wrong.

"A business," writes Golomb, in *How to Find, Capture and Keep Customers* (Raphel Publishing, Atlantic City), "is not a business if it doesn't make a profit. It fails. *The purpose of being in business is to get and keep customers.*"

And to do this, he says, you need to realize the value of each customer.

To determine this value, figure out the average dollar amount each customer represents in sales per year by dividing sales by the number of customers, he says.

Then, according to Golomb, you can use this key figure to strategize. For example, if each customer is worth an average of $80, adding 300 customers to an active customer list would mean an increase in sales of $24,000.

Despite being so "simple and so obvious," he says, this crucial calculation eludes many — even though recognizing the value of each customer is "basic and fundamental" to success.

"A customer is worth far more than the immediate sale," he says. "Each customer is gold."

With that thought in mind, let's take a look at the sometimes difficult task of qualifying — finding out each prospect's potential for you and your company.

No one believes more strongly in the premise that time is money than salespeople working in the field. It seems strange, then, that an investment of time in searching out and qualifying leads that help to expand sales is treated so lightly by so many salespeople.

Reasons for this lapse aren't difficult to identify, however. A list of reasons would certainly include some of the following:

- Searching out leads by salespeople can be chancy at best.

- Many men and women in sales are confident time can be better spent contacting and servicing regular customers.

- Screening out positive leads from those with little or no potential can take away from more profitable activities.

- Incentives are lacking for screening and obtaining leads from the field.

- Leads from company headquarters may be ill-timed, out-of-date, or mailed to salespeople on a haphazard basis.

- Prospecting takes care of all lead requirements.

Sometimes leads that come to salespeople from their companies — or leads they obtain on their own — fail to provide the information they need. For instance:

- Is the lead from a specifier? Influencer? Decision maker?

- Is this prospect near a buying decision? Does he or she have a specific service, product, or application in mind? Or is the prospect merely window-shopping?

- Who else within a prospective account that is soliciting information should be contacted? Or receive literature?

- Is this solicitation worth a call? If so, when? Within what time frame — right now? next week? in a month? maybe a year from now?

Are there steps salespeople can take to overcome this impasse? While there are no guaranteed, sure-fire solutions, there are some practical procedures that are not difficult to implement.

Many valuable sources are available for use in obtaining leads in any given territory. Because of the number of sources available, you have the option of picking and choosing the method that will produce maximum results in minimum time. In general, these lead sources can be divided into two categories: those you get personally and those provided by the company for which you work.

Typically, *personal lead sources* will encompass:

- *Cold canvass* within specific areas of your territory, in which information is obtained concerning names and addresses of companies, lists of management personnel, types of businesses, products/services produced, and so on.

- *Publications* to determine lead possibilities such as telephone directories, chamber of commerce literature, data from government agencies, and so on.

- *Territory exposure,* in which you get tips; observe personally; listen to comments; and check for new construction, changes in business ownership, personnel changes, trade and newspaper stories, bankruptcies, and so on.

- *Direct referrals* received from present customers, friends, and other regular contacts.

- *Reworking lost accounts.* These "orphans" frequently are prime suspects for a planned lead-development activity, as is detailed in chapter 3.

- *Working a specific category of business.* Sales personnel select a certain business category existing within their territory and subsequently investigate it intensively for lead possibilities.

Leads developed by progressive, profit-oriented companies may frequently include such sources as:

- *Inquiries from interested parties* who voluntarily contact companies for information about products and services. Or they may be from those who respond directly to a company's advertising, public relations, direct mail, or community contact activities.

- *Company-wide lead prospecting* in which designated members of the sales management group conduct frequent, intensive lead-development activities. Through this activity it is possible to identify and account for more types of businesses that are potential customers than through a random system that hits or misses in seeking out possible leads.

In developing a lead-finding procedure, simplicity and ease of use are major priorities. The following suggestion can be put to work quickly and effectively.

Begin by plotting the boundaries of your territory on a map. The map (a road map will usually do nicely) should be big enough to pinpoint identified leads and prospects. It should also allow you to plan your coverage of these leads as well as your regular accounts.

Next, mark with a colored pen or pencil the location of prospects you've already identified and classified. They may be organizations you're either working on now or plan to contact in the near future.

Develop a *written master list of leads* you have found, recognized through published sources, observed while covering the territory, or that have been identified for you by your company. Be sure to add new lead possibilities as they become available. Locate these potential customers on your map as well.

Finally, begin planning contacts with leads you have determined are worth cultivating. As you develop your plan, cover these details:

- Determine whom you will see, including names, titles, degree of authority. Add basic background facts you have worked up concerning his or her personality, as well as identified wants, needs, and requirements.

- Develop priorities. What objectives must be achieved on your initial call? On follow-up and subsequent calls? What must your planning encompass in order to make your objectives a reality?

- Prepare a schedule of contact after deciding the frequency with which this new account should be seen. Estimate when the first order can be anticipated.

- Integrate these new lead contacts into your regular coverage of the territory.

- Create a list of questions to ask during a call on a prospective account. They may concern:

  — The account's general business objectives

  — Specific information concerning the operation and management of the organization

  — Facts about the strengths and weaknesses of other suppliers who are also competing for the lead's business

  — Additional information not known before the call covering the lead's needs, wants, and requirements.

If there was ever a time when a systematic approach to getting qualified leads for salespeople was needed, it is now. That's why every step of the lead-development process must be handled with care — especially the last step, *follow-through*. Facts surrounding the call should be noted, including methods used to penetrate the account successfully, additional information to be obtained, and possible next steps to implement on future calls.

A careful after-call evaluation will also identify others within the prospective account to contact on future calls. Equally important, the true value of this new prospective account can be accurately calculated, as well as the steps to follow to bring it into the fold.

PROBING FOR PAY DIRT

The questions you ask of a new account are vitally important to your sales relationship. When you don't quiz a prospect about needs early on, you risk putting him through a nightmare.

Consider this scenario:

A woman wanted to learn about cash surrender options on her insurance plan. But, when she visited her investment advisor, she was slammed with a heavy-duty sales pitch about a new savings/retirement program.

The sales rep plunged into his presentation with only the shallowest of background checks, learning only what insurance plan the woman now had and that she was retired. Then he took off with his spiel about a "finer financial future."

The prospect was polite—until she saw what was going on. The she became by turns disillusioned, uncomfortable, irritated, and then angry. Finally, she blurted: "This is ridiculous! You're trying to sell me a complex program without knowing anything about me at all!"

Who could blame her for her outburst?

Had he inquired, the self-centered rep might have discovered that the prospect, although retired, had a substantial income from a trust account and was a sales consultant of national reputation. Indeed, she was far from a normal prospect. Not "just a retiree," she was a person of special professional qualifications. If the rep had asked some key questions—and listened to the answers—he would have tailored his presentation in a far different manner.

But all chances of a sale were lost when the prospect got up and walked out. Don't let this happen to you!

- **Prepare yourself for effective probing by doing your homework.** Find out as much as you can about a prospect before the first meeting—no matter how difficult it is. Delve into clippings and biography material.

Search out associates, employees, and friends of the prospect to talk to.

- **Make your questions good.** Your queries do more than inform you. They also alert the prospect to possibilities and options.

Good questions transform listeners from passive absorbers of information into active participants in the sales process—the kind of prospects who become customers. Good questions pull prospects out of their shells and get them into the spotlight, where the prospects can be examined. Good questions also force sales reps to listen and avoid overtalking.

Have you analyzed your probing skills lately? It's worth the time.

Remember: While a prospect is answering a well-put question, he or she can't possibly be saying "No sale."

SIZING UP A CORPORATION

You probably spend many hours personally getting to know new prospects before you make your first attempt to sell to them.

But what about corporations? How do you size up a complex organization?

The best way is to create a "sales profile" for each company you pursue. You can do so by answering the following questions:

- *Size.* What are the firm's annual sales and profits? How many full- and part-time employees are there? How does the corporation compare in size with similar corporations?

- *Ownership.* Is the firm family owned? If so, who controls the policy and sets the tone for corporate activities? If the company is not family owned, is ownership concentrated in a few individuals or divided among thousands of stockholders?

- *Management.* Who are the key players on the firm's senior management team? How long have they held office? What are their educational and professional backgrounds?

- *Product/service line.* What does the corporation sell? What is its full product line, including after-sale products and services? The lines offered by subsidiaries?

- *Customers.* Who buys from the corporation? What attracts customers? How are products or services sold?

- *Branches.* Where does the corporation do business? In a single location? At branches? Are the facilities owned or leased?

- *Uniqueness.* What makes the corporation unique? What distinguishes its employees or products from those of its competitors?

- *History.* Who founded the corporation? When? How do the company's origins influence its business philosophy today?

- *Corporate culture.* How would you describe the corporation? Progressive? Traditional? Energetic? Thoughtful?

- *Buying cycles.* When does the corporation need the products you offer? Do seasonal factors affect need? Economic or social factors?

A sales profile, built from annual reports and other printed information, newspaper clippings, and even idle chatter, can tell you much. Through it, you can get to know the corporation well before you launch your first sales presentation.

Then, armed with solid, up-to-date information, you can begin your sales presentation with confidence and vigor.

TOO MANY LEADS

Put yourself in this position: You've hustled for months on a personal lead-generation campaign. But now you realize that you can't possibly pursue all those leads thoroughly.

The alternative to this hopeless task is a systematic "qualification campaign." By taking time to qualify your prospect, you'll be able to determine where and how you can most profitably spend your time.

Each of the following techniques can work well in your qualification campaign:

- *Customer analysis.* Which of your leads most closely resemble your existing customer profile? Consider the demographic, social, and economic characteristics of your best customers, and you'll be able to build a prospect profile.

- *Industry profiles.* Your trade association might offer composites of "typical" customers. See if you can match the profile of a typical customer with some of your leads.

- *Self-qualification.* By telephone or survey, you can pose simple questions about the buying habits and volume of individuals on your lead list and narrow the list down to a manageable size.

- *The Delphi technique.* Modeled after ancient Greek fables, the Delphi technique uses several "great" minds to arrive at a clear conclusion about an issue. Using this technique, you can sit down with a few of your colleagues, review your lead records, and decide which leads you should pursue.

- *Cost-benefit analysis.* What 20 percent of the individuals on your lead list are likely to spend the most money on your product or service? Which individuals on the list represent the greatest potential for increased sales growth in the future? Cost-benefit analysis suggests that you spend a significant amount of time developing these leads.

- *Current buying habits.* At the time you place targets on your lead list, find out where they're spending their money right now. You might choose to give high priority to individuals served by a weak competitor or multiple competitors.

- *Intuition.* While intuition is hardly a scientific decision-making technique, don't discount its value. In fact, the more experience you have in selling, the more likely your intuition will help you accurately pursue high-quality leads.

- *Direct questions.* In this age of "empowerment," many employees are empowered to do everything *but* make buying decisions. Use direct questions to find out whether your prospects *do* have buying power. Ask:

  — "Did *you personally* choose your current vendor?"

  — "How long have you been with the company?"

  — "Are you a principal of the company?"

  — "Who else is involved in the decision-making process?"

- *Requalify prospects during your first appointment.* When you first meet a prospect, offer your business card and ask for his or her card. Is the person's title on the card? Is it the *same* title the prospect mentioned when the two of you first had contact? If it isn't, you're looking at a red flag. If the title *is* the same, compare this prospect with some of your current customers — not just as a businessperson, but also in terms of overall personality.

Ask yourself:

— Does this person ask the same kinds of questions as my current decision-making customers?

— Does this person *act* like any of my decision-making customers?

— Does this look like a person who can buy from me *right now*?

If the answer to any of these questions is "no," chances are you're talking to the wrong person.

• *Make the best of any bad situation.* If you find you've made a mistake by not properly qualifying the person you end up calling on, make the best of things by probing deeper into the company's needs and wants. Find out who does what. Show a few samples, but don't try to *close* this person! Thank the person for his or her time and, on the way out, ask: "Oh, by the way, could you introduce me to the decision maker you mentioned before I go?"

Based on what you sell, the time you spend qualifying a prospect will depend to some degree on the possible payback. For example, if you're selling earth-moving equipment, considerable time may be spent determining not only the specific types of equipment used, but also the prospect's ability to pay.

On the other hand, if you're selling long distance telephone service by phone, you can't afford more than a minute or two per prospect.

If what you sell fits the latter category, a faster and simpler method is in order.

THE QUICK-QUALIFIER TECHNIQUE

By using the "quick-qualifier" technique, you can reduce prospecting time by learning up front which prospects are worth pursuing. Here's how you can make the quick-qualifier technique work for you:

1. **Admit that you have no relationship with the prospect.** "We've never met," you might open. Or: "I know you don't want to spend time with someone you don't even know." Or: "I know I'm not on your calendar today."

2. **Introduce yourself — candidly and directly.** Without fanfare, let the prospect know that you regularly canvass for prospective customers and that you're doing so now. For example, "I'm with the Jones Company, and each year I try to make at least 200 cold calls on people who might need my products." Or: "Your name's on my list of prospective customers, and I try to call each name once a year."

3. **Offer your benefit in a sentence or two.** Let the prospect know what you're selling by noting benefits. You might say, for example, "I specialize in selling lighting systems that reduce energy costs." Or: "I offer equipment repair services, and I emphasize fast turnaround."

4. **Give your prospect an out.** Subtly force your prospect either to invite you to tell him or her more, or to end the conversation. Say: "I know you're busy and I don't want to go into any more detail unless you think I might be able to help you."

5. **Await the response.** Your prospect will respond in only one of three ways:

   If he or she says, "No, I'm not interested," you can thank the person for his or her time and indicate that you'll check back next year. The prospect will appreciate your brevity.

If the prospect says, "Tell me more," you have an opportunity to offer a brief description of your product and, if necessary, set an appointment for further discussion.

If the prospect says "maybe," you can prod until you get a commitment to talk again or an indication that the person's not interested right now.

Whatever happens over the course of your quick-qualifier calls, you've covered a lot of ground in a short time. Within just a week's time, such calls will save you an enormous amount of time — time you can now spend with your best prospects.

QUICK TIPS

- Concerning cold calls, make it a point to discover what method works the best for you in "getting a foot in the door" — whether it is working the phone, writing letters, or getting referrals from satisfied customers — and then *concentrate* on that method.

  Whatever method you choose, however, always be sure to state your case concisely and politely.

- Never lead with your product. The secret to getting to and persuading decision makers is to "keep your product in your pocket." You need to talk about the critical issues facing the buyer and the capabilities needed to meet those issues. Remember that a product should always be what the buyer visualizes as the *solution* to a business problem.

- Prospects first want understanding — who they are, what they do, and the problems they face. Only then can you determine if and how your products or services fit their needs. Being a "strategic partner" is critical in today's selling environment, but requires a thorough understanding of the world the customer lives in.

- Create a relaxing climate. It's a fact: *Relaxed* prospects raise fewer objections than nervous prospects do. Nervous prospects do everything from questioning price and available alternatives to wondering out loud if they even need what you sell.

To get your prospects to relax, learn as much as you can about your prospect before your first meeting and then appeal directly to your prospects' interests.

- Sales trainer Bill Bishop offers these thoughts about prospecting:

    — "Prospecting is a contact sport."

    — "Your output depends on your input. A high input of prospects will give you a high output of sales."

    — "Suspects are unqualified bodies of ore. Prospects are qualified veins of gold. Rejects are disqualified, worthless rocks."

    — "Without a prospect, you're unemployed and out of business."

WHAT WOULD YOU DO?

I waste a lot of time calling on the wrong person — one who doesn't need my product or doesn't have the authority to buy. Any tips on how to qualify prospects?

The qualifying process demands patience and brain power. Make sure you follow these basic steps:

1. Conduct a thorough study of your company's best customers. Look at how these customers use your products and the benefits they enjoy from the applications.

2. Call on prospects in the same industry or who might have the same applications as your customers. By doing this, you can employ your expertise and knowledge of the jargon of the trade, as well as gain immediate attention by telling success stories.

3. Develop a profile (including rank and title) of the ideal buyer. Spell out in some detail a description of your target customer.

4. Develop a dialogue in which you gain the favorable attention of the prospect. You need to do this before you can ask qualifying questions.

5. Use tactful qualifying questions to fit the prospect to your "ideal buyer" profile and to determine if more than one person is involved in the decision-making process. Don't mow prospects down by asking questions one after the other like a prosecuting attorney. Use your own words and weave the questions into your dialogue. To make sure you're talking to the final decision maker, ask whether he or she makes the decision on this kind of purchase or whether others are involved. Also determine whether there is real interest and adequate money available.

SUMMARY

One reason so many salespeople give up trying to find new accounts is their unwillingness or inability to qualify prospects properly. The unfortunate result is a lot of wasted time with little to show for it.

To qualify a prospect, you must clearly identify a need and ability to buy.

You need to go through your list of all possible prospects in your territory and ask yourself if each has a possible need for what you are selling — and why. This, of course, means you will have to do some homework on every prospect in terms of learning about the business of each one. This exercise alone will start you preparing a good sales presentation tailored to individual cases.

You'll probably come up with three categories of prospects: those with a strong need, those with a lukewarm need, and those with little or no perceived need.

You must determine early on the potential sales and profit of each prospect, as well as your chances of making the sale. On the latter point, be careful that you don't make a judgment too early. The old expression "His bark is worse than his bite" fits many situations. Just because the buyer is a bit grouchy on the first call doesn't mean that he or she won't buy from you. In fact, many salespeople will tell you that they love to call on buyers who have scared off all their competitors! It makes their job a lot easier.

When you get down to the basics, qualifying success depends largely on knowing what questions to ask and not being afraid to ask them. Success comes with experience. The more you do it, the better you get.

CHAPTER 5

MAKING APPOINTMENTS

You know that getting an appointment is half the sale. You've got to use your best selling techniques just to get in the door. So don't hold back your most effective moves; put yourself in gear and give it your all.

You're confident you can sell that prospect. You have a great product, demand is good, and you're a seasoned salesperson. But the prospect is tough and clearly reluctant to see you. What do you do to get over that first hurdle?

The prospect probably has his or her working day carefully planned. When you ask for 30 minutes of the prospect's time, you are asking for a considerable portion of his or her day. You must give a good reason for the prospect to make room to see you.

Here are some tips:

- *Be open to your prospect's suggestions.* Your prospect may be willing to see you at a certain time or on certain terms. But if you're too rigid, you may not get your chance.

- *Get some help.* Do you know someone who can open that door for you? Perhaps a mutual friend or acquaintance? (See chapter 2.)

- *Give prospects an incentive.* No one wants to waste time. But a prospect might meet with you if he or she sees some advantage for doing so. Think of an offering that might interest your prospect. Don't lean on vague generalities or make wild claims you can't substantiate. Instead, appeal to the prospect's curiosity and interests.

- *Indicate that you'll be in the area on a certain date.* People may not want to meet because they don't expect to buy, and they don't want to send you on a wild goose chase. But if you let them know you'll be in the area anyway, you'll remove their apprehensions.

- *Promise prospects that you won't pester them.* People also dread hassles. They don't want to sit through a badgering session or get pestering calls after the session.

- *Tell prospects what you'll cover.* Prospects who have an idea of what you'll cover may be less apprehensive. Send them a summary of your presentation. This marks you as an efficient professional with a clear agenda.

- *Assure prospects that you won't take long.* Prospects may fear being inconvenienced or bogged down by windy salespeople. Assure them that you will need no longer than a specified (and brief) period of time.

GETTING IN THE DOOR WITH A MINI-APPOINTMENT

The next time you have trouble getting an appointment for a formal sales presentation, ask for a mini-appointment. Here's how it works:

1. When you visit a hard-to-schedule prospect, acknowledge to her secretary that you know that she is very busy and that you're *not* interested in making a sales presentation at that time.

2. Instead, note that you would like to show a 30-second display to your prospect, personally present her with materials, or explain one simple fact about your product line.

3. You can even suggest to the secretary that you're noted throughout the community for this brief and efficient presentation technique. If you say this, of course, be sure it's true!

4. At this point, it's the rare secretary who will shut you off. If the prospect you're trying to reach is truly busy or unavailable, the secretary may give you some advice on the best time to make a mini-appointment — or perhaps even schedule one for you.

5. When you get in to see your prospect, present your material exactly as you promised. Don't take any more time than the prospect expects you to take.

6. As your mini-appointment draws to a close, summarize your comments, present your business card, and leave.

In practicing this method, remember one key thing: Your purpose during a mini-appointment is not to make a sale.

It's not even to make a formal presentation.

It's simply to make a brief, but memorable, contact with a prospect — and to distinguish yourself as an efficient sales rep who sincerely respects customers' precious time.

In this day and age of sophisticated marketing, this novel, low-key approach to getting your foot in the door will stand out from more "pressure-oriented" tactics.

While your mini-appointment won't result in a sale, you can be sure that it *will* set the stage for formal presentations and discussions later on.

These suggestions are invaluable for getting in to see the routinely overworked, overscheduled, overburdened prospect, but what about those legendary big buyers who will not see *any* salesperson?

IF YOU WANT TO LEAVE A MESSAGE

If the person you want to see is not in, you may in some instances set your own appointment for later in the day or the next day. The secret is to get the buyer's secretary, assistant or switchboard operator to agree to this, and to pass the information on.

For example, you can say, "I'm sorry I missed Susan Jensen today. Would you please tell her that I will call on her tomorrow morning at 10:00 a.m." Leave your name and company, and depending on the situation, leave a phone number where you can be reached.

If you call back for the second time and find that the buyer is out, tell the person you're talking to that you have tried to contact the prospect a number of times with no success. Ask what is the best possible time to call and tell the person you are talking to that

you would appreciate having the message conveyed that you will call tomorrow at a specific time. Relating your frustration and nailing down a specific time will improve your chances of contacting the prospect.

WHEN YOU WANT A DELAY

For one reason or another, you may want to delay seeing your prospect. You may need time to prepare your presentation, you may need a concession from management, or you may want to assemble testimonials. You don't want to give the customer the impression that you are too busy. The best way to do this is to call when you are sure he or she is going to be out. Call before he arrives for work, at lunch time, or when you know that she will be in a meeting. Say that you are difficult to reach over the phone and that you will call later. This puts you in the position of appearing to make efforts to contact your prospect with very little risk of actually doing so.

These suggestions are invaluable for getting in to see the routinely over-worked, over-scheduled, over-burdened prospect. But what about those legendary big buyers who will not see *any* salesperson?

HOW TO SEE THE NO-SEES

Who are they? They're the "no-sees" — prospects who have repeatedly said that they will not see you *or* your competitors.

Why even bother with a no-see, when you have other prospects who *will* see you? Because many no-sees are *very large* customers who can greatly reward your efforts.

Salespeople who succeed with no-sees are those who approach obtaining that first interview step-by-step — just as they'd approach getting their first order from a prospect who *will* see them.

Example: You've repeatedly visited the headquarters of a large supermarket chain that doesn't stock any of your products. The receptionist calls the appropriate buyer, who says he won't see you because he's not interested in your product line. Several attempts by telephone go nowhere. What do you do? Here are some options:

1. **Collect information.** Discover what you can about the buyer from the buyer's assistant, a receptionist, and others at headquarters. Ask: "Does he give other salespeople similar treatment?" "Just who does he see?" "What advice can you give me about trying to reach him?" Then talk with several store managers. Ask them about the buyer, as well as about their own business challenges.

2. **Establish communication with others.** Visit headquarters regularly and be pleasant with everyone. Always leave a brief handwritten note for the buyer. Don't be afraid to ask for help. Remember: Your immediate objective is to get a personal interview. You will be amazed at how many people will help you when you *ask* them for help. Ask questions to determine if there have been any changes in the "no-see rule" since your last visit.

Do not leave samples or literature unless the buyer has specifically asked for them. Even then, try to get the OK to deliver the samples in person. Never give samples to the receptionist or other personnel. Instead, leave inexpensive favors, such as cookies or candy.

Always attach a personal note to *anything you leave* for the buyer, even if it's just a business card.

3. **Be persistent.** Patience and persistence are your strongest allies. In selling, nothing is final! If you're in the area monthly, call monthly. Never show frustration. Continue to be friendly while making it clear that you don't give up easily. Most everyone has a positive feeling about salespeople

who believe strongly in their products or services. If you haven't had the experience of getting in to see a no-see and coming out with an order, you have something to look forward to. It's a great feeling of accomplishment.

IMPROVE THESE RESULTS WITH THESE SIX TIPS

1. Be prepared. Know what you're going to say. Be confident. Work from notes, including a checklist so you won't miss any important point.

2. Use a conversational tone. Speak naturally, as you would face-to-face. Think of yourself as smiling and happy. Visualize the person on the other end of the line being the same.

3. Identify yourself right away. State your name and who you represent slowly and clearly. Try to get the prospect to remember your name, "This is Fred Hartman, just like that expensive Hartman luggage, except my prices are better." "My name is Fran Rogers, no relation to Mr. Rogers, but spelled the same way."

If your name is difficult to pronounce or spell, laugh and say something like, "I don't care what you call me as long as you call with an order."

4. Be sure you pronounce the prospect's name correctly. If in doubt, ask. Use it several times during the initial discussion, but don't overdo it. Using it at the beginning of every sentence is upsetting to most people.

5. Ask questions. If you are not sure you understand everything the prospect says, or if you feel that you may have missed a point, ask for a clarification. If you don't clear this up now, it may embarrass you later. When you want a customer to elaborate on a point, pursue the point by using a reflective phrase, such as "you said," "you mentioned," "you cited before," or "you described." After repeating the statement, follow through with a question beginning with who, what, when, why or how.

6. Be a good listener. You won't always reply directly to what the prospect says, but you can't give the impression that you are ignoring her comments. Listen carefully and courteously. Concentrate. Focus your mind on what the customer is saying. Practice shutting out distractions. Limit your own talking. You can't talk and listen at the same time. Don't interrupt. Even a long pause doesn't mean that he has finished saying everything he intends to. Don't jump to conclusions. Avoid making unwarranted assumptions about what the customer is going to say and avoid mentally trying to complete her sentences.

GOOD WORDS AND BAD WORDS

A good vocabulary can be a big asset when you are trying to make an appointment with someone you don't know. Choose words that are precise and easily understood. Here are some useful and some not-so-useful words and phrases:

Words that build rapport:
- I appreciate your problem
- Let me try to be more clear
- That's really great
- I like what you are doing.

Stimulating words:
- Discuss
- Evaluate
- Let me explain
- Will you help me?
- What is your opinion?
- How do you feel about..?

Words that build interest:
- This system will...
- Unusual application
- Distinct benefits
- Unique idea

Words that create distrust:
- To be frank
- Honestly
- I want to be candid
- Truthfully

Words that alienate:
- Do you understand?
- No kidding!
- Get the point?
- Tell
- Point out
- I'll tell you

The idea is to create sufficient interest to get an appointment without actually giving your pitch over the phone. Select words that fit the prospect's situation or need, such as "additional sales and profit," "saving time and money," "new," "guaranteed," and so forth.

DEALING WITH THE DOWN SIDE

How many times in your sales career has a prospect not shown up for an appointment? How many times have you worked for months nurturing a sales relationship only to find out that your prospect wasn't really the decision maker? While these problems are more common to new accounts, they are by no means limited to them. How can you prevent these incidents?

Sales managers and sales trainers typically label these occurrences as "rejection," which "comes with the territory." However, if you have ever driven two hours to an appointment to wait an hour in a reception area only to find out that your prospect can't see you — you realize that a career in sales can indeed be demoralizing. Feeling "rejected" because a person doesn't need your product is acceptable to the psyche, but feeling "humiliation" because a prospect doesn't treat you well is an entirely different ball game.

You must deal with your temporary loss of dignity psychologically before you can move on to the next prospect. If you can discuss the incident with other salespeople, you will find that something similar (or perhaps worse) has happened to them and this will soften the blow. Before you run out and quit what might be a very profitable, rewarding, and challenging sales career, stop and build your self confidence.

As a salesperson, you are an expert. No one knows your product or service and its uses and benefits to others as well as you do. You also know your market, its needs, its economic situation, and the competition. In fact, with your information you can help your prospect solve problems so well that you are actually a consultant in your area of specialty (your product or service.) Now you have to go one step further — you have to establish to your prospect (as well as yourself) that you are indeed a professional.

How does professionalism help? Think about your last visit to the doctor for a physical. You made an appointment, marked it on your calendar, arrived at the office early, waited half an hour, let the doctor poke and probe you, thanked the doctor, and paid the receptionist on the way out. You did the same thing at the dentist's office, and a visit to a lawyer would have a similar scenario. Salespeople don't usually command the same authority as doctors and lawyers, but you can attain a level of respectability that will make you and your prospective client comfortable.

There are some consultants who actually charge prospective clients to meet for a sales appointment. They can do this because there is a value to their time and expertise. Even though you can't necessarily charge for your time and expertise, you can convey the value to your prospects and earn their respect.

In order to convey professionalism, you have to be a professional. Understand the signals you send out from the moment you pick up the phone to the "thank you" letter you mail after your sales meeting. Your appearance, your manners, your handshake, even your voice indicates who you are, and how much you are worth to the prospect.

Here are some other cues that are important to maintaining an aura of professionalism as you work through the sales process:

1. **Never lie to your prospect.** Your ethics are as important a tool to the sale as your product is. Don't say you will take only five minutes of your prospect's time when you know you will need fifteen. Not only will you lose the prospect's trust that is key to any sale, but also you will convey a lack of integrity — something professionals strive for.

2. **Set a firm time and date for all your appointments.** When you set your first appointment with a prospect, specify a time and date for your meeting. Don't say, "I'll be in the neighborhood—why don't I drop in?" Or "Whatever day is good for you." This shows that the prospect is important, but you aren't.

Instead say, "I have an opening on Tuesday at three, or Friday at 11." This indicates that you are an equally important person with other engagements, and would like to meet with the prospect at your first available opening. If that time is not convenient, offer another time and date, but don't let your desire to secure an appointment make you sound desperate.

3. **Arrive for your appointments on time.** Arriving very early puts time pressure on the prospect, and arriving late indicates a lack of respect for the prospect's time. If you must be late, call your prospect and explain; it eases the tension that lateness can cause and is actually the same common courtesy you expect from him.

4. **Don't wait longer than 15 minutes for an appointment to show.** Besides making you angry (and anger will lose the sale), waiting alone in a reception area is uncomfortable for both you and your prospect. To avoid the embarrassment, leave before everyone in the office knows you better than your prospect does. The difficulty is, however, leaving in a professional manner. Control your anger. Leave your business card and explain to the secretary that you can't wait any linger but will be glad to reschedule at a more convenient time.

5. **Present your business card and ask for your prospect's as soon as you meet.** Not only does this help your prospect remember your name, but it also sets the tone that two professionals are meeting to work on solving a problem. Always keep your cards with you and offer them freely.

6. **Be prepared to speak well of your prospects as well as your competitors.** People move around from company to company and chances are that the person you are meeting may be friends with others you have worked with. Therefore, it is far better to speak positively of people than to risk alienating your prospect with negativity. Also, when

a prospect speaks of one of your competitors, compliment the competitor and then turn around the objection. You don't want to verbally destroy a company your prospect has worked with for years.

7. **Don't become the receptionist's/secretary's best friend.** Sometimes salespeople overrate the importance of friendship with the prospect's secretary. Befriending the secretary will not get you in to see the prospect if he or she doesn't want to see you. Be friendly and cordial to everyone you meet in the prospect's office, but concentrate your efforts on the prospect and the sales relationship.

8. **Don't telephone your prospect too often.** Persistence is crucial in sales. However, the salesperson who calls repeatedly when the prospect won't take the call tends to get blocked further. When you are trying to reach a person, call once in the morning, and if it is important, once again in the afternoon.

If you really find yourself abused often in the field, it may be that your attitude and behavior may indeed invite the abuse. On the other hand, if once in a while you encounter a situation where a prospect is hurtful to you, move on. There are plenty of other sales opportunities available so that you shouldn't have to put up with severe abuse.

None of the tips above will guarantee you a "humiliation-free" sales call. Many of those uncomfortable incidents are a result of the prospect's lack of common courtesy, the traditional fast talking "salesperson" image, and the fact that we don't always have the sales relationship we think we have with a prospect. However, if we behave like professionals—we will become professionals.

This confidence alone will help to shield us against the mistreatment we sometimes face in sales.

QUICK TIPS

- Sometimes very busy buyers will see you outside business hours, usually early morning or late afternoon. Not everyone works nine to five especially doctors, small business owners, and individuals involved in 24-hour operations, such as transportation, communications, and public safety.

- When all you can reach is an answering machine or voice mail, remember to:

  - *Speak clearly and slowly.* Rushed, garbled messages are confusing and often unintelligible. How can you expect someone to return such a call?
  - *State the reason for your call.* If you need specific information, request it. Then the person can have it handy when returning your call.
  - *State your phone number* at both the beginning and the end of your message. This allows the person to locate your phone number quickly and easily without having to search for it.

- When making appointments, don't overlook your company's or your product's news value. Use comments like "Did you see the story about our new drug in yesterday's *Wall Street Journal?*" or "Our company just received the coveted Baldrige award." Good news sells.

- Getting past the gatekeeper. Here's help in keeping you "well connected." When you call, immediately

give your name and that of the person you're calling on. This prevents the gatekeeper from saying,
"May I say who's calling?" and implies that the target person will recognize your name.

WHAT WOULD YOU DO?

I pride myself on being organized and try, whenever possible, to call in advance for an appointment with a prospect. The problem is that although I'm punctual, often my prospects are not. This really throws off my schedule — and my planning. Any ideas on how to tackle this problem?

There are a few approaches to this problem depending on the individual situation. Generally, buyers strive to keep appointments. However, buyers are subject to the internal demands of their organizations, and internal meetings and/or projects scheduled to be completed before your arrival can stretch out beyond the control of the buyer.

If there is a legitimate reason for a buyer not to make your appointment on time, there is probably nothing you can do but wait — especially if it is an important call on which an order will be obtained, a complaint must be taken care of, or you have some vital information you must get to the buyer.

Perhaps some gentle nudging of the buyer's secretary, without being obnoxious, can shorten your waiting time. Secretaries usually know what's detaining the buyer and may even be able to get the buyer out of a situation he or she would prefer not to be in.

After about a 10-minute wait, you might approach the secretary and, glancing at the clock, say something like: "Gee, I know that (buyer) really wanted to talk about (or see) the figures I have and I want to spend the necessary time with (buyer). But I have another firm appointment 30 miles from here at (time). Can you see if (buyer) can see me now?"

Even if the secretary does nothing more than check with the buyer and communicate your story, it will make the buyer conscious that you have been waiting. This should induce the buyer to get out to see you sooner.

You might also gamble and tell the secretary that your call's important, but that you're going to have to leave in about 15 minutes. Mention that if the buyer isn't available, you may have to delay this important meeting to another time. This will either get you some quick action or you'll have to reschedule the call.

If the call really isn't important, wait about 15 minutes, then announce to the secretary that you can't wait any longer and reschedule the call.

This approach should impress the buyer with the importance of your time, and perhaps for the next appointment the buyer will be available at the scheduled time.

However, in the case of crucial calls or calls on buyers who habitually keep you waiting, the best strategy is to phone the buyer ahead of time and reconfirm the appointment.

SUMMARY

It's more difficult than ever to make appointments today. With downsizing, many organizations have cut their buying staffs to the bone.

There was a time when you could count on private secretaries and switchboard operators to at least tell you why you couldn't get an appointment. Now your call either goes directly to the buyer, or you're faced with a recorded voice that asks you to select one of several options, none of which (usually) gets you very far. Or you're supposed to know an individual's extension number, but, of course, no one bothers to tell you, or no one that you finally reach will tell you.

While the busy buyer may have good reason to turn on his or her voice mail when arriving at work in the morning and leave it on all day, it doesn't mean that you have to accept it. Many salespeople today are using other means to reach the reclusive buyer:

- Walking in without an appointment
- Using mail, fax, and overnight delivery or messenger service
- Going over the buyer's head.

These measures may seem extreme, but remember, you won't sell anything unless you reach the decision maker.

Fortunately, getting in to see many buyers and decision makers is not difficult if you'll follow even a few of the ideas shown in this chapter and in the next, "Improving Telephone Skills."

A few salespeople have the attitude that they're doing the customer a favor simply by showing up once in a while. This attitude is unacceptable. Just because your company sells products or services that customers want and need is no reason for such behavior.

Like the sales presentation itself, making appointments requires a variety of approaches. Using the same failed approach over and over again with the same prospect is like hitting your head against a brick wall hoping that the bricks will eventually fall. Many have tried it. The only thing that happens is that your head will develop a definite ache.

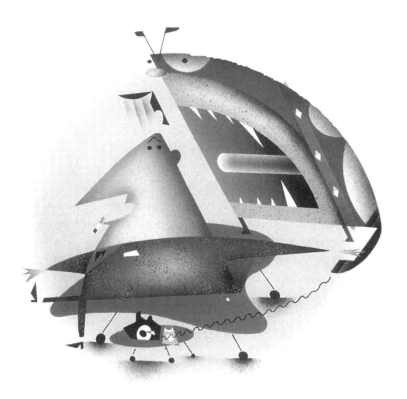

CHAPTER 6

IMPROVING TELEPHONE SKILLS

Within only a few decades after Thomas Edison said, "Come here, Watson, I want you," into his primitive invention, the telephone became vital in business. Today the telephone is one of the most important communication tools any salesperson uses. It is especially necessary when selling new accounts, because getting that first appointment by phone requires a great deal of skill. Good telephone skills are critically important to your success.

Used with skill and understanding, the telephone can be a powerful — and ultimately profitable — sales tool. It helps you contact prospects, make appointments, and pave the way for the first face-to-face interview. It's essential to your success

Prospecting by Phone

Place a couple of warm-up calls before you start your calling for the day. Call other departments; check on inventory, order processing, and overdue accounts, and so on. Just as athletes warm up their muscles before competing, you can prepare your voice so it can perform at an optimal level.

Develop a warm and friendly rapport through your attitude and voice so you attract favorable attention. Psych yourself into knowing that you have the right to speak, that you have a product or service the person you are calling needs or should have, and that he or she definitely will want whatever it may be.

Exude self-confidence. Adopt a matter-of-fact attitude. Consider yourself to be on an equal basis with whomever you are calling. Put authority in your voice.

Plan each call you make as carefully as you plan your in-person visits. Before phoning a prospect, learn as much as possible about the prospect's company so you can create the feeling that you're calling a friend who needs what you have but just doesn't know about it.

Never start talking without first identifying yourself. Specify the goal of the call, then outline how you intend to achieve it. Get right to the point. Use your prospect's name as often as you can without seeming to overdo it.

Get leads at your library

The library is an excellent source of leads for telephone solicitation. Reference books highlight large users of your product in your territory of which you may not have been aware. Many ref-

erence books give information such as telephone numbers, size of business, and even the name of the contact for you to call. A few of the better-known reference works are *Dun & Bradstreet's Handbook, Moody's Industrials, Thomas' Register,* and *Standard and Poor's Register of Directors and Executives.*

Professional and trade lists are available at the library. These lists allow you to target in on a particular area. You may want to concentrate on one particular market, in order to become a "specialist" in that business. Industry journals are also available, and reading the articles is often as valuable as extracting the names of companies that advertise in the journal.

Various other publications may be appropriate to your industry. Perhaps government papers or government publications might be of interest. If you are making a trip out of town to see one or two customers, The Yellow Pages can be invaluable.

When cold-calling from your list of prospects, don't skip around if you run into a streak of bad luck. Unless the entire list is flawed, you should be persistent and call every name on the list. Remember that the next name has absolutely no relationship to the rejection you encountered on the prior call. Also, do not prejudge a prospect by the name or location. The huge account you are looking for may be that next call — even if it has an unappealing name, or is in an undesirable part of town.

BEFORE THE CALL, DO YOUR HOMEWORK

Because of the increase in calls from poorly trained telemarketers, many prospects — and even established customers — have become wary of unwanted calls and are more careful to screen them out. Your challenge, then, is to try to gain favorable attention and stand out from the crowd.

When telephoning for an appointment, you must make the prospect want to see you. Remember that when you ask for a 30-minute appointment, you're requesting one-sixteenth of the average working day. That time will not be granted unless you can sell the *value* of the visit.

As we mentioned in chapter 3, before you dial your prospect's number, make sure you do your homework. Investigate your company's records of your best customers.

Find out how these customers use your products and what benefits they enjoy from their use. You'll get more attention if you tell the success stories of other companies that have used your product or service.

Your prospects want to know *why* they should talk to you, and your homework will help you show them. This is when your homework pays off. By briefing them on your work with other organizations in their industry, you develop interest and should be able to convince them to make an appointment with you.

After you've identified the prospect as a qualified buyer, pique his or her interest by suggesting that you have a product or service that will improve efficiency, cut costs, enhance profits, or whatever single benefit you can get across in a short phone call. Don't try to dump the full load.

When you get an interested response, immediately set up an appointment. Suggest two alternative dates and times, such as: "I'll be in your area Monday and Wednesday of next week. How about 9 a.m. on Monday or 2 p.m. on Wednesday?" If neither is convenient for the prospect, he or she will suggest an available time, and you're in.

When you send literature to prospects after an initial call, mark or stamp on the envelope in large red letters, "Here is the information we discussed by phone." This will set the package apart from other materials they receive, and they'll open it more quickly.

AVOID TELEPHONE TAG

Most salespeople know the frustration of playing "telephone tag" — wasting valuable time by calling and re-calling prospects and customers.

Avoid telephone tag by planning your calls more effectively. Research shows that you can greatly increase your chances of making that important connection by calling in the morning from Tuesday through Friday.

In conjunction, there are many reasons why calls are not returned promptly. Prospects may indeed lack interest in your product — but they also may be under time or work pressures.

Avoid building your sales day around expected incoming calls. It doesn't make sense to adjust your schedule on the basis of what you expect the prospect to do. Instead, retain the initiative on phone contacts — and prevent frustration.

End the Runaround from the Blockers

Sometimes when you're pursuing a good prospect, you run into the telephone "blocker." Although some blockers may be assigned by your prospect to filter callers, others are self-appointed authorities.

How do you handle them?

The first step, according to Joan Guiducci, national speaker on prospecting and author of *Power Calling — A Fresh Approach to Cold Calls and Prospecting* (Tonino), is to put blockers at ease.

Guiducci suggests testing the waters. Say to the blocker, "I didn't know you made those decisions for the company. How do you fit in? . . . Maybe we should meet." Say this in a light way, without arrogance, and you'll probably avoid any bad feelings.

In your mind, separate *gatekeepers*, who are merely screening calls, from *blockers*, who usually don't have the authority to stop your calls.

Circumvent blockers when you can. And know when to walk away. But be persistent, and things may go your way.

Also, beware of the blockers who beat their own drums. When you come across a blocker who says the company "relies on my advice on these issues," ask questions that the blocker can't possibly answer. For example, you may ask, "How have you solved the problem of maintaining a constant oil flow to that critical bearing?" This reduces the blocker's self-appointed authority, and you'll usually be connected with your prospect.

Don't forget to treat the blocker with respect — you can't bully your way through.

Just explain your goal and work diligently to recruit the blocker to take part in your quest. Keep in mind that you need all the help you can get to reach the prospect.

GETTING PAST THE GATEKEEPER

You know that meetings with decision makers make sales possible. But to gain these sales opportunities, you must have an appointment. That means getting by the decision maker's "gatekeeper" — the assistant or secretary who answers the decision maker's phone and screens calls.

Dennis Fox, president of The Client Development Institute, Reston, Virginia, points out that "the gatekeeper is not employed to get rid of people, but to make sure that the right ones get through. You must convince him or her that you are one of the right people."

But before you convince the gatekeeper, you must first convince yourself.

Feeling that you are the "right person" is a state of mind, Fox says. You must believe that you are equal in rank to the decision maker and that he or she needs to see you.

That confidence comes through in your voice when you talk to the assistant.

But you don't need a course in assertiveness training to project this confidence. A few simple tactics will often get you past the assistant and through to the person you want, Fox says.

To begin, when the assistant answers the phone, speak politely and mention your name first:

"Hello, this is Donna Martin. Is Mr. Grabert in?"

By placing your name first, it sounds as if you know Mr. Grabert and should be connected immediately. You won't sound like a typical salesperson.

This direct approach is so unusual that it may cause the assistant to ask for your name again. Politely and softly say, "As I mentioned, this is Donna Martin — *thank you.*"

Be sure to put the "thank you" at the end, without a pause, and then say nothing else. This "no-pause-thank-you," as Fox calls it, says that you are an important person, you should be put through, and you're ready to talk to the person in charge.

About 70 percent of the time, the assistant will put you right through. He or she won't want to keep someone important from talking to the boss. Of course, a few assistants may continue to question you. They may ask, "Do you know him?" Your reply: "We haven't met, *thank you.*"

If he or she persists and asks the nature of your call, have your homework ready to go! For example, the easiest call to make is when you have a referral, enabling you to turn a cold call into a hot call by saying, "I'm calling about some work I've done with Mr. Jenkins at ABC company, who suggested I call Mr. Grabert, *thank you.*" However, if you don't have a referral, a cold call can still be turned into a warm call using the "Like-with-Like Principle": "I'm calling about some work that we've done for presidents of other small wholesalers in the Delaware River Valley, *thank you.*"

Once you've been connected, you can let your sales ability go to work on the decision maker to set up that appointment — the original reason for the call.

STAY COURTEOUS

Pushy telemarketers, insistent fund-raisers, frustrating voice-mail systems, and rude employees pushed to the limit by corporate downsizing — these and other forces make for a growing incidence of telephone rudeness.

This atmosphere makes it tough for you, as a courteous, sensitive salesperson, to use the phone to conduct business.

But don't react by using bad phone manners yourself. Face the tension on the phone line and do your part to inject some peace into the situation. By "losing your cool" on the phone, you risk instilling resentment in the people at the other end of the line — and losing business as a result.

Take heart in the fact that quick brush-offs from prospects might be a reaction to the avalanche of unwanted calls by poorly trained salespeople and telemarketers, and that the rude handling of incoming calls, as well as the failure to return calls, often stems from overworked employees. Overcome these hurdles by being patient and tactful.

Once again, remember not to let frustrations with voice-mail systems get the best of you! Realize that such technology is often misused. Go with the flow and do your best to get your message across — and gently remind prospects that voice mail often hurts companies by screening out useful sales propositions along with irrelevant ones.

And while we're talking about voice-mail systems, you might listen with a critical ear when you call your own company to retrieve your messages. Do your prospects or customers have to jump lots of hurdles to access your voice mailbox? Not all innovations are progress. A pleasant-voiced, competent receptionist can provide a welcome contrast to the typical "press 7 now!" commands at too many businesses.

QUICK TIPS

- Develop a list of key questions to ask a new client over the phone.

- Take charge of your phone conversation and stay on track.

- When making calls, always speak in a relaxed, friendly manner.

- Try to be in a good mood when making your calls.

- Occasionally tape-record yourself on the phone to judge the impression you're making.

- Speak slowly and clearly to avoid irritating the listener.

- Before making your calls, eliminate all distracting background noises.

- Keep your calendar and appointment book close to your phone.

- Ask prospects and customers if it's a convenient time to talk with you.

- Be certain of your prospect's name and how to pronounce it before making your call.

- Be polite to everyone with whom you speak.

- If you're running late, call your next appointment with an update.

- Make sure your office knows how to reach you with any important messages.

- Make sure customers always know how to reach you or where to leave a message for you.

- Check your messages regularly and return customers' calls promptly.

WHAT WOULD YOU DO?

Our company is a well-known manufacturer representative firm covering four midwestern states. I have almost no trouble making appointments with existing accounts, but recently my supervisor has asked me to make at least one prospect call each day. When I call for an appointment, I'm usually told to send literature or that the prospect is not interested in our line. What should I do?

If cold calling is new to you, and your comments suggest this, I would, in addition to reading everything in this book, ask your supervisor to demonstrate his or her skill with this type of call and recommend additional reading.

Ask other salespeople, especially those in your own company, for suggestions.

It's quite possible that prospects know the products you sell better than they know your company, so be sure to mention both when calling.

Above all, don't give up. It takes a lot of practice to become good at telephone solicitation, particularly in these times when it seems that just about everyone wants to do business by phone.

If you've not done so, try stopping by the offices of some of your prospects and asking to see the appropriate person(s). You may find that this is more effective than telephoning. Although the buyer may not be able to see you when you drop in, he or she may give you an appointment for a later time.

SUMMARY

One of the first things a salesperson learns is that talking on the telephone requires a somewhat different set of skills than talking face-to-face.

A second lesson is that talking with a prospect who doesn't know you is not the same as talking with one who does. And it can be a whole lot more difficult, too.

The more that all of us use the telephone, the more we try to protect ourselves from too many incoming calls. To help us cope, technology first gave us the answering machine, then computer-controlled voice mail.

They've been so helpful that we tend to overuse them — and therein lies the problem. What salesperson has not said, "If I have to listen to another phone menu, I'll scream!"

Since prospects are not likely to change their appointment procedures any time soon, we have to learn new ways to cope. This book and particularly this chapter provide a number of ideas that will definitely be useful for improving telephone skills. Give them a try.

Remember that just because you have difficulty making a telephone appointment doesn't mean that the buyer doesn't want to see you. It may simply mean that he or she is having difficulty coping with an overcrowded schedule and a telephone system not of his or her choosing.

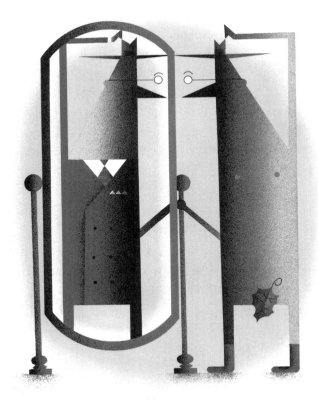

CHAPTER 7

WHAT TO SAY ON YOUR FIRST CALL

Whether you have an appointment with a prospect or simply walk in for the first time, what you say and how you conduct yourself will have much to do with your future success.

These days, what call isn't "cold?" Downsizing, mergers, bankruptcies, and other corporate casualties have put customers once thought to be cast in bronze in a definitely chilly category. And that's not all that's changed.

Buyers and other contacts you once knew intimately have been either forced into retirement, into business for themselves, or are doing for someone else what they formerly did for your old customers. New people have emerged with requirements yet to be crystallized.

Chances are, you're making more calls on new people than you once did. First impressions are lasting ones. Be courteous but businesslike. Project an air of importance. Consider everyone you meet as being important, and suggest that you have important things to talk about.

Remember names and use them. Pass up no opportunities to meet people. Let them know whom you represent.

As you know, the more knowledge you have about a prospective customer, the better. If you walk in with little or no knowledge, obtaining the information will be your first priority.

Many professional salespeople will visit the office of a prospect that they know little or nothing about simply to size up the situation and collect information. They do not ask to see the buyer. They tell the receptionist that they've stopped by to see if the operation purchases the types of products or services they sell. They ask questions like, "Does your company use a cleaning service? What company serves you now? Who is responsible for handling this service? Does she work by appointment?"

What these pros have learned is that if you say you don't want to see anyone or sell anything to them today, it's much easier to get information. This approach sometimes works when you telephone the prospect. You say to the switchboard operator or the buyer's secretary, "I'm not calling to make an appointment with your buyer *today*, but can you tell me what days and hours she sees salespeople?" Once you get this information, you may be able to get additional information about the buyer, such as how long she's held the position, plus information about brands and quantities of products purchased that are similar to yours, or any other information you'll find useful not only when you see the buyer, but also when you try to get an appointment at a later time.

In most offices or places of business that you're visiting for the first time, you have a better opportunity to size things up than you do when telephoning. Usually the first person you'll meet will not be the decision maker you want to see. This gives you an opportunity to quickly collect information that will help you when you do talk with the decision maker, or to decide that this is not a worthwhile call.

After stating your name and company, ask questions to determine potential, for example:

- "Do you ever employ temporary help?"
- "What positions are covered in this way?"
- "Who's responsible for this?"
- "May I see him now?"

Most times you can quickly determine if it's worth your time to go further, but be careful — the person you see first may be instructed to get rid of all salespeople that are not on the "accepted" list. Therefore, don't take everything at face value. Also, the person you first see may not have enough knowledge about purchases to answer your questions. In this situation, try to talk with the top person in the department that has responsibility for the types of products or services you offer.

Again, the same rules that apply to telephone appointments apply to personal visits. Don't give your pitch to anyone who can't make a buying decision, and don't give your business card to any intermediary, who can then say, "I'll give your card to the decision makers. They'll call you if they're interested."

WHEN TO LEAVE QUICKLY

You may simply want to have someone to call on because it beats the boredom of working on the telephone. Fight the temptation and be sure that all of your prospects are properly qualified. During the sales call be especially attuned to whether or not this is a legitimate prospect. If the prospect is strictly killing time, only interested in price, or does not have the money in their budget for your product or service, terminate the conversation as quickly as possible and leave.

Just look at your watch, say you must be going, and do so.

WHAT DO PROSPECTS NEED TO KNOW?

How much does a prospect need to know? That depends on the salesperson, the prospect, and the offering. In general, the more the prospect knows about your offering, the more inclined she will be to buy.

But it's not always that simple. While it's important to mention key selling points as soon as possible, it's also important not to overwhelm the prospect with too much detail. In short, there's a certain amount of information that a salesperson should provide his prospects at any given time.

How can you tell how much information to provide your prospects? Consider these points:

- **Organize.** Know exactly what you're going to say. Rather than going into too much detail right away, use your initial contact to explain a couple of key points. [Remember, you have something to offer your prospects that either provides them a benefit or helps them prevent a loss. Therefore, you plan before the presentation to gear everything you say to achieving either or both of those two objectives].Then, tailor these points to your prospect's emotional interests. Use your follow-up calls to elaborate on details pertaining to your initial presentation and to add secondary appeals.

- **Prepare your prospect before your meeting.** The more your prospect knows about your offer, the less talking (or even selling) you'll need to do. Consider sending her some advance information to pave the way for your visit.

- **Ask.** Take advantage of your initial questioning period to determine your prospect's specific needs. That will enable you to know which matters you should address first and to what extent you should cover them.

- **Draw your prospects out.** One way to limit your direct questions is to draw your prospects out. You might do that by making provocative statements, such as: "All my customers tell me that this system has helped them to double their productivity." That statement not only makes a powerful sales point, but it will almost certainly entice the prospect to ask how the new system can do that.

- **Don't give too much too soon.** Some people are easily overwhelmed by new information. Organize your presentation into compact segments. Begin with a few basic points. Concentrate on those points until your prospect has digested them. Move on to other material only when you need to. Keep in mind that you don't necessarily have to cover every point during your initial meeting.

- **Fill your prospects in completely.** While you don't want to give your prospects too much information too soon, you still want to be thorough. Balance those two objectives by sharpening your message to its barest essentials. Develop a presentation that covers all essential information in relatively few words.

- **Show and tell.** Don't rely entirely on your words. Always provide your prospects with plenty of visual materials. By supplementing your message and by providing your prospect with a useful reminder after you've completed your call, your handouts will enable you to concentrate your verbal presentation on the more vital points. Remember that the most effective visuals are simple and understandable at a glance.

- **Observe.** Analyze each sale you make. At what point did your prospects agree to buy? How much did you need to tell them? What exactly did you say? Learn from your past successes.

GET PROSPECTS TO BUY NOW

The salesperson had just made a fine presentation. Everything went as she had planned, including asking for the order. But instead of saying, "Fine, I'll take it," the prospect said, "It looks good, and it's probably what we need, but I want a little more time to think it over." Sounds like a reasonable request, so the salesperson should pack up and hope that he'll tell her later when he's decided to buy, right? Not if the sale is important to her! Professional salespeople don't risk losing a sale to a competitor who just happens along later if they can persuade a prospect to buy now!

Why do prospects resist? People resist buying for fear of making a wrong choice and getting blamed for a poor deal. They may be reluctant to change a habit, or just hate to make decisions. Frequently they are nearly convinced they should buy and wish the salesperson would help them make the decision. Don't let them down!

The usual methods for overcoming resistance and closing sales will work for the prospect who want to think it over. Find out why he wants to wait. You might ask, "Why do you think you should wait?" or "What is it you feel you need to think about?" The answers might disclose a misunderstanding you can correct. If it's just plain reluctance to make a decision, here are four ways to get action:

1. **Describe the advantages of buying now.** Point out the benefits he agreed he would receive starting now. Why wait? Bring out other advantages like a sales price, prices going up, limited supply, increased prestige.

2. **Describe the problems of waiting.** While these are comparable to the advantages, they might be more forceful in the negative. Examples: higher costs, lost time, bad results, higher cost later, dangers of status quo.

3. **Offer inducements for buying now.** Review the advantages over competition. Consider special inducements like something free—a gift, an accessory, trial period, installation, delivers. If there is a special discount, mention it, but don't depend on cutting prices.

4. **Reduce the number of decisions needed.** Too many choices often cause the prospect to put off the whole purchase in frustration. He just wants to get away. Help this prospect by reducing the choices to two. "You seen to prefer these two models." Put the rest away and ask, "Which one do you like the best?"

TURNING A LEMON CALL INTO LEMONADE

Mike Walters has learned to expect anything to happen on any given sales call. He'd spent a lot of time trying by telephone to get an appointment with the purchasing agent at a new plant that had just opened in one of the far corners of his territory. Like the plant, the purchasing agent was new, and he was being bombarded by reps in all industries trying to get in to see him.

Walters says, "One of my problems was the plant's location. It was pretty well off the beaten path for me. Frankly, unless I could make this a major account, it wouldn't be worth my while to pursue it."

Walters continues: "For about a month I kept up my telephone campaign. Finally he agreed to an appointment and we set one up for the following Friday. The reception I got wasn't what I expected: The purchasing agent had been called out of town on an emergency. So it looked like a wasted trip. I couldn't stay over the weekend — I had several important calls set for Monday.

"In desperation, I asked for a tour of the plant, and that was the turning point. I saw example after example of how my company's products would fit right in. I made notes and sketched a few diagrams showing how and where the operation could be made more efficient. Next, I talked with a few of the employees so I could get a feel for the company. By the time I finished, I had plenty of ammunition for my next visit.

"Then I thought, 'Why not write up all my recommendations and leave them for the purchasing agent to look at Monday morning?' That was the real payoff.

"The agent was so impressed with my analysis that it gave me a real edge over the competition — just because I refused to see the entire day wasted. And there was an added benefit: Because I had done my homework, the agent raised very few objections during my presentation. Because of my initiative, he truly wanted to do business with me."

Not every sales rep has Mike Walters' experience and creativity, but we can all work toward his level of ingenuity.

Consider Contacts by Mail

Some individuals respond favorably to a first contact by mail. This gives them information in a no-pressure situation and will help obtain your first appointment. Listen to what distinguished sales expert Robert F. Taylor, president of Sales Counselors, has to say on the subject.

One of the important tools of selling, making contacts with prospects and customers by mail, is too often neglected by salespeople. Selling entirely by mail is reserved for specialists in direct-mail advertising and promotion fields. Professional salespeople, however, frequently use the mail as a supplement and reinforcement of their face-to-face calls, particularly on first-time calls.

Brief notes of formal business letters mailed in between your sales calls, can serve as additional "sales calls." They can help you maintain the momentum you built up during the sales interview. They can further develop your image as a true professional, one who is sincerely interested in the prospect's objectives. Messages by mail can do the following:

1. Help you get your foot in the door

2. Convey additional information.

3. Remind the prospect of commitments made

4. Confirm appointments or agreements

5. Ask for additional information

6. Thank or compliment the buyer

7. Make catalogs and sales brochures stand out from other promotional literature received by the prospect.

Be informal

Many salespeople avoid using the mail because they believe it requires a formally written business letter. In some cases, a well-composed, informal letter is more appropriate. In many cases, however, a brief, handwritten note will suffice. In fact, the handwritten note provides the opportunity to put some personality into the message and to help develop the friendly atmosphere you are trying to create.

It is smart to present your name to the buyer as often as possible. This must be done tactfully, without becoming obnoxious. Brief, handwritten notes can accomplish this. Their informality will not offend the buyer; they can be quickly written by the sender and easily read by the receiver; and they get the job done.

A good example of the effectiveness of the informal note is when the prospect asks you to send some sales literature. Some individuals consider catalogs or brochures "junk mail," and throw them out. A handwritten note, however, attached to the same literature will be placed on the top of the stack for the immediate attention of the prospect. Your personal message will make your catalog stand out and demand favorable attention.

Build an Image

Your business correspondence produces a tangible reflection, not only of your personal ability and knowledge, but also of your organization's image.

Your company spends considerable money on advertising to promote its products and to create a positive image. This image can be negatively affected by carelessly prepared correspondence. If there appears to be no pride in something as basic as business correspondence, it follows that there is little concern for quality of product or service. Conversely, well-written messages that convey style, expertise, and sincere interest present a good image.

There is more than one good corporate image as it applies to correspondence. One is the image projected by the formal business letter. It should indicate sophistication, class and dedication to excellence.

The second image is that of a friendly, sincere, consultative salesperson. This is also a good image, created by timely, informal notes to prospects and customers on subjects pertinent to their needs. Develop and maintain both these images.

Five building blocks

Letters that sell the product, arrange a meeting, get an appointment or get some other desired action that could lead to a sale are called selling letters. They must be planned and composed as carefully as you would plan a sales call. If you haven't already done so, take a course or read a good book on business letter writing to help develop a good writing style that gets the message across effectively, without unnecessary words and hackneyed expressions. For your sales letters, think in terms of these five building blocks.

1. **Gaining favorable attention.** After the usual salutation, write a paragraph designed to gain the reader's attention. A powerful selling sentence, for example, is a good attention-getter.

2. **Holding interest.** Hold your prospect's interest by expanding on the opening sentence. Add additional benefits.

3. **Making the proposal.** Give a clear, concise explanation of your proposition. What do you want the prospect to do and why should he or she do it?

Perhaps all that you want is that first appointment.

4. Handling objections. You can't hear the objections, of course, but you can anticipate some from your experience. Make strong points that will allay the prospect's fears.

5. Asking for the desired action. You have a clear objective for the letter: an appointment, a purchase or some other desired action. Ask for it!

Finish your letter with a complimentary close, without using undue flattery.

One of the keys to all sales contacts is good planning, and this is particularly true for the business letter that is designed to sell.

FIRST CALL JITTERS

It's not unusual to feel anxious or nervous on your first call. There are, however, some things you can do about it. Here are a few tips:

1. Learn as much as you can about the prospect *prior* to the call.

2. Prepare your presentation before the call, and practice it.

3. Arrive a few minutes early, and review all your notes before entering.

4. Check to be sure you have all the necessary samples and presentation material.

5. Look your best. It builds confidence.

6. Consider what the prospect may ask and be prepared with answers. Know your customer's mind-set. By being alert, you can learn a great deal about the mind-set and personality of your new buyer. Your approach should be designed to get a better understanding of how your customer oper-

ates. For instance, is the customer precise, meticulous, and demanding? Is the customer open to new ideas? Knowing that a customer procrastinates or likes to take charge of a situation can be invaluable when serving the new account.

7. Be prepared to mention a fact or two about the prospect and his or her organization. Draw out the customer. Ask questions to learn about his or her goals, quality specifications, pricing targets, and service requirements. Be conversational. And don't create animosity between you and the customer by using pressure tactics.

8. Make at least two positive or complimentary statements during the first five minutes.

9. Provide proof that what you're saying in your presentation is true.

10. Exude confidence.

11. Be friendly and smile.

12. Visualize a successful call, all the way through to a successful close. Coordinate yourself. Awkwardness and fumbling with paperwork are not the ways to get on well with a new account. By proper planning and practice, you can exhibit smooth coordination in all your sales actions.

13. Transfer the ownership feeling. You'll gain points in your presentation by making the prospect feel like an owner. Say to the prospect or customer, "Wouldn't you be proud to have this in your inventory?" or "Wouldn't you like to be the owner of one of these products?"

14. Be diligent in handling complaints and difficulties. If, in the opening stages of your relationship, it becomes necessary to handle complaints, make sure your response is quick and decisive. Act with extra effort and dedication.

Your primary goal in serving new accounts is to discover what is needed to stay on favorable terms with the buyer. Once you determine these points, your future customer relations will proceed smoothly — and profitably.

Remember that being a bit nervous is natural and can be a good thing because it keeps you on your toes. Also be aware that your prospect may be a little nervous, too.

FIRST CALL ICEBREAKERS

When it's really important that you see a prospect, you may have to use some extraordinary measures. In his book, *State of the Art Selling* (Career Press), Barry J. Farber gives three examples:

1. A business machine salesperson enlarged his business card on one of the copiers he sells. This not only got lots of attention, but also enabled him to demonstrate a product feature.

   "The receptionists would ask how I made the enlargements," he says. "Of course, that would lead me into explaining the enlargement feature. It got the interest going, and soon I was known as 'the guy with the big business card.' Often, receptionists would put the card on their bulletin boards."

2. An industrial supplies salesperson wanted to have an uninterrupted conversation with an important prospect away from that person's office, but couldn't persuade the person to get away. So the salesperson sent a chauffeured limousine to whisk him away to a restaurant.

   This approach was so successful that she uses it regularly.

3. During a special new-accounts campaign, a salesperson for a floor and ceiling manufacturer sent prospects a letter of introduction followed by a Federal Express package announcing that he would be calling the next day.

   The impression was that the sales call must be important if it was announced with a FedEx. Results — 90 percent of the prospects agreed to and kept the appointment.

Perhaps you have an icebreaker or two that work for you. If not, develop a few. Select something that fits you, your personality, and the type of prospect you're calling on. You may hesitate to use an icebreaker that's out of the ordinary, but remember that whatever you do, your objective is to gain attention and be remembered. Passing out key chains won't do it.

One salesperson we know carried a three-legged milking stool with him. Before starting his presentation, he would place the stool on the buyer's desk. When the buyers asked about it, the salesman would say, "Our prices are higher than some of our competitors, but we give you two other benefits — high quality and excellent service. Each leg of this stool represents one benefit: price, quality, and service. Some competitors offer two of these benefits, but our company is the only one to offer all three." Then the salesman would remove one of the legs. The stool would fall over. Years later customers still remember the three-legged stool, mention it, and laugh. But it worked.

OVERCOMING CUSTOMERS' FEARS

Many salespeople fear interacting with customers—especially new customers—for a variety of reasons. The people they are about to see may be rich, powerful, influential, or intellectual giants. This could put all but the most confident salespeople on edge.

What most salespeople fail to realize, however, is that frequently customers fear salespeople. Let's look at some of the reasons for this, and then study how we may overcome those fears. Here are a handful of reasons, presented in random order:

1. **Customers fear you may sell them something they don't want, don't need, and/or can't afford.** Most likely, customers who feel this way have been stung before and don't want it to happen again.

2. **Customers fear you may take too much of their time.** This is especially true if they've scheduled other appointments throughout the day. Sometimes this worry causes customers not to see you at all.

3. **Customers fear you may not deliver on your promises.** This is especially true if you and/or your company are new to them.

4. **Customers fear they may offend you.** People prefer to say "yes" rather than "no." And few enjoy intentionally hurting anyone.

5. **You may be too overpowering.** Maybe you've got a loud voice. Maybe you are quite physically imposing. And maybe you don't take "no" for an answer. All these things can and do frighten customers.

6. **Customers may have had a bad experience with you, your company, or the products you represent.** This may be why they reject your overtures to visit with them.

7. **Customers may be giving their business to others.** Nobody likes change for the sake of change. They may fear you for the changes you might force upon them. Few people willingly leave their comfort zones.

Now, let's look at how you can cope with these fears: You can easily overcome fears No. 1 and 2 early in your presentation by saying something like: "Ms. Prospect, I won't sell you anything you don't want, don't need, or can't afford. I don't operate that way. That's why I'll need some additional information, so we can mutually decide on this. I'm only going to take 20 minutes of your time, unless you want me to stay longer. And we may conclude that I don't have anything that interests you. Can we get started?

To overcome No. 3, show testimonials from customers you've pleased. Don't worry about No. 4, because that's your customer's problem, not yours.

To overcome No. 5, speak softly; wear dark clothing if you're larger than most people; avoid wearing large, noisy jewelry, and so on.

Overcoming No. 6 requires additional probing. You need to know the exact problem your customer encountered in the past before you can formulate an answer.

And to overcome the fear described in No. 7, you should come up with sound reasons why dealing with you, rather than your competitor, will pay off.

QUICK TIPS

These six tips, from sales expert Jim Rapp writing in *Personal Selling Power,* can increase your chances of success with prospective customers.

- *Follow up immediately* on all leads.

- *Qualify the prospect early* to determine volume and profit.

- *Establish your reputation* and your company's during the first visit.

- *Do more information gathering than selling* on the first call.

- *Identify at least two customer needs that your company can fill* that are not being satisfied by current suppliers.

- *Don't make the first call a "do or die" situation.* Leave the door open for future visits.

- *Handle new accounts with "A-B-C."* The ABCs of customer contact will mean fewer roadblocks:

    Approach — Give your customer that favorable inner feeling about you.
    Balance — Don't be too aggressive; on the other hand, don't be overly friendly, either.
    Conviction — Demonstrate your products and build desire.

- *Be alert for prospect problems!* Ask questions during fact-finding calls and listen closely for problem areas. Follow through — do your homework and present a full answer. Problem solving leads to business.

- *Remember that all-important first impression!* Remember the "three-thirty" rule: The prospect forms an impression of you in the first *three seconds* — and you have to work *thirty minutes* to change it. Be yourself. Use a positive, natural opening — and look 'em in the eye. Make your first "three" really count!

WHAT WOULD YOU DO?

I've found it fairly easy to make appointments, but I do have a problem developing any kind of rapport with buyers on the first call. What can I do to overcome this?

Developing good relationships depends, in great measure, on *your* interest in the person you're seeing. Most people can tell if you're really interested or just faking it. Listen with your eyes as well as your ears.

Psychologists tell us that if you make a sincere effort to get to know an individual, even though your initial reaction is negative, you will have a better feeling about the person over time. More important, the other person will sense your interest and will be more open to you.

When you meet the prospect for the first time, get into that person's world *immediately*. Look around the prospect's desk or work area. What do you see? A diploma, an award, family pictures, indications of a hobby or other interests? These things provide opportunities to talk about the prospect's favorite subject — him or herself.

The more you learn, the better able you will be to focus on the prospect's professional and personal needs.

A new, young pharmaceutical salesperson was having difficulty bridging the generation gap between herself and the much older doctors she was visiting. She not only felt inferior, but also believed, incorrectly, that the doctors had no interest in her or her generation. She felt awkward asking questions about their medical education and work experience, which sometimes had occurred before she was born.

After attending a sales training course her company offered, she learned that:

1. The age difference offered an opportunity for her to ask questions about the medical profession over the years. After a while, she was able to sharpen her questions to

the point where they provided a perfect lead-in to the kinds of prescription drugs she was promoting.

2. Most of her clients had a positive attitude toward her generation and women in sales positions.

3. Her clients' discussion of the history of treating specific diseases enabled her to use this information when talking to other doctors, particularly young doctors.

She also learned, quite by accident, to ask expectation questions. On first calls, at the appropriate time, she said, "This is my first visit with you. I want to make these visits as helpful to you as I can, so please tell me, what do you expect from me?"

A doctor might answer, "Honesty and up-to-date information." The salesperson would then say, "Don't stop there — that's just one expectation — are there others?"

She learned that expectation questions have several benefits: First, she quickly learned the doctors' ground rules for these calls. Second, she learned what interested them as far as her products were concerned. Third, she flattered the doctors with questions that most other salespeople never ask.

You may not sell pharmaceuticals, but these techniques will help you develop rapport quickly with any buyer. Remember, focus first on the prospect, his or her company, and problems they're having that might be solved by your products or services.

SUMMARY

It would be a wonderful thing if you always received an order on your very first call. We know that this is not a realistic expectation, so don't use all your ammunition the first time around.

Depending on what you're selling, it may take you three, five or ten calls before you get that first order. Don't let the disappointment of that first turndown keep you from going back.

Remember that each call is a building block toward the first and possibly many orders to follow. Also keep in mind that your degree of success will depend primarily on your ability to determine each prospect's needs, then match your products and services to those needs.

You must be interested in the person *and* the problems. About the only way to accomplish this is to listen, ask questions, and **learn**.

The more first calls you make, the better you'll become at them.

CHAPTER 8

SUCCESSFUL PRESENTATIONS

What do salespeople do for a living? We change things. We bring companies and people new and better ways of doing business. We bring progress. We improve the human condition by bringing more effective and efficient machines and methods to the world.

But on our first contact, our prospects know we have come to ask them to change. We want our prospects to see us as a source of help and welcome us as partners in progress. Why do they attempt to avoid us? Could it be that the nature of mankind is not to look for opportunities to change? Do people prefer to remain the same?

HOW TO BEGIN CLIENT RELATIONSHIPS

So many of us call a prospect for the first time and get a flat-out rejection. Why don't prospects want to talk to us? Why do they brush us off? Why do they view salespeople as threatening? Often we start out, even with the best intentions, saying:

- "We have a better way"
- "We'll help you improve"
- "You'll do better with our product"
- "Our method is an improvement over the way you do things now."

Our customers, however, can interpret our opening statement as a criticism or insult. They might be hearing:

- "We don't think you're doing very well"
- "You need help"
- "We're here to show you the right way"
- "We're here to change you."

SHOW PROSPECTS WE APPROVE OF THEM

How do you react to people who say things like this to you:

- "You've certainly been successful"
- "Well, what you are doing is certainly working"
- "You are the industry leader"?

By the same token, don't prospects like to show us how well their companies operate?

- "I don't know as much as I'd like to about the tool and die business. You certainly have done well. Could you show me around and point out the major factors contributing to the success of your business?"

And when our prospects see that we appreciate their abilities and success, that we approve of them, we can say:

- "You know, you mentioned your scrap rate is higher than you want. Would you be interested in cutting your scrap rate and possibly reducing production time as well?"

And at that point we can discover how our products can help our prospects.

Beginning can be the hardest part of the sale. It's easier when the prospect sees us as supporters and not critics.

Pre-Approach Planning

It's been said that the close begins with the pre-approach. It makes sense. In fact, there is a series of steps that lead from the pre-approach to the close. And each of those steps takes careful planning, preparation, and execution. Unfortunately, salespeople often neglect the pre-approach. When the work in that area is not performed or is sloppily handled, it can start a chain of errors that can seriously affect the sale.

You must ask yourself a series of questions prior to your first call on your prospect:

- "Whom are you going to see?"
- "What is your objective for this call?"
- "What are you going to present?"
- "How are you going to present it?"
- "Why should the prospect buy?"

- "What visual aids will you use?"
- "What testimonials will you use?"
- "What success stories will you use?"
- "What objections do you expect?"
- "How will you respond to them?"

These and similar questions force the sales rep to think out prior to the sales call all the things that are likely to happen during the interview. This is sometimes called "creative imagery." It's a good way to plan every possible detail — and certainly helps to develop the professionalism that is so vital in selling.

Most buyers are very busy, and they are very conscious of the importance of time. They therefore appreciate the planning and preparation evidenced by the smooth approach this pre-planning permits.

Prospects with ambitious long- and short-range objectives are inclined to buy from salespeople who bring them bold, dynamic, creative ideas: recommendations, suggestions, and new product applications.

Willy Loman, that quintessentially unsuccessful rep in Arthur Miller's play, "Death of a Salesman," proclaims that to be good in sales one needs only a smile and a shoeshine. In the real world a sunny disposition and natty appearance are the expected. Smiles and shiny wingtips go with the territory.

If these were the only factors sufficient to close sales, computers or a well-oiled robot could probably function successfully in almost any market. Fortunately for most salespeople, management has yet to discover how such devices might be programmed so that they have the exact knowledge necessary to understand a customer's problems, needs, and objectives.

While personal appearance rates high—no question about that—even more important are the sales presentation skills called upon to relate a product's applications to an account's wants and requirements.

Too often the temptation is to make a swift pitch and depart. Pressures of time may be one reason. The number of customers to be seen in a day could be another. Or perhaps it is simply impatience to get on with it that blinds some reps to real sales possibilities waiting to be seized.

Whatever the reasons, such slapdash efforts are costly, resulting almost always in a lack of interest on the part of buyers. And orders range in size from zero to embarrassingly miniscule.

What does it take to make calls produce worthwhile results?

Whole libraries have been devoted to this single subject. But to prevent time-wasting groping in the dark, here are some practical pointers.

- When prospecting or contacting relatively new accounts, look for organizations that are growing and changing in the particular business or industry served by your company. Working with winners is somehow always easier than peddling to also-rans.

- Check the trade press. Make contact with non-competing reps who also call on these customers for business. It is one of the least expensive techniques for quickly becoming acquainted in a field about which you may know little. More important, information picked up permits you to talk knowingly about your products and/or services in terms of the customer's business requirements.

- Find out the names of those who play roles in either deciding, influencing, or specifying the buying decision. It may take one or more phone calls or personal contacts to reach these people. But, in the end, less time will be wasted traipsing from office to office seeking someone authorized to buy.

- Before making a call, a careful rehearsal of what you plan to say, show and do is every bit as vital as a football team's final runthrough of plays before a big game. The rehearsal should also include reasons why an account might turn you down. A list of cogent responses can then be developed in the presentation to help overcome resistance or obstacles to the sale.

Every buyer expects sales reps who call to be great talkers. It's part of the mystique. But be careful! The temptation to overwhelm buyers with the exuberance of one's verbosity has done more than its share in killing off sales than, perhaps, anything short of cold-blooded murder.

The essential trick is to stimulate the customer's interest—and ensure her attention. Doing so requires the presentation to be limited to those product features and functions of special benefit. Attempts at impressing the account with an encyclopedic knowledge of what it is you sell or service not only confuses, it may also effectively stall the decision to buy indefinitely.

It's a safe bet competitive comparisons will be raised sometime during a typical interview. While the traditional response is never to downgrade others also seeking the business you are after, it is also little help to pass them off with praise, however faint. It's also little help to treat competitive products as though they didn't exist.

Instead, grab every chance to identify reasons why your products are better. Focus on their strengths. Stress areas of clear superiority. Introduce unique differences that guarantee savings in time and dollars. If possible, try to close the deal once the account signals agreement with the comparisons you have offered.

One of the great mysteries in sales is, why after making an impressive presentation—even taking away a signed order, further contact with an account is dropped. (At least until the next time around, maybe weeks or months later.)

Is there a better way to demonstrate your continuing interest in a customer than by calling when you know she is not ready to buy? We're not talking about time-wasting idle chit-chat because you happened to be in the neighborhood. We're talking about stressing opportunities in which you can:

- Offer solutions to problems revealed during previous calls;

- Check on deliveries or billings;

- Review new products or services about to be introduced to the market;

- Suggest a time or money-saving procedure observed during calls on other accounts;

- Ask about ways you or your company can assist the customer in his quest for growth and profits.

Sales success rests on the way you address your desire to be of service. Communicating your concern for a customer's welfare and the means used to solve problems are two of the surest ways to elbow competition out of the picture and cement long-term relationships.

On a practical note, your personal help and recommendations can have a snowball effect. Bigger sales are not the only result: your customers' recommendations to others are likely to follow with very personal benefits to you.

Setting Call Objectives

Most calls offer possibilities for achieving several objectives. Major ones are easy to identify. Problems, if any, usually occur when determining the order of their preference. A simple strategy is to define one or more maximum objectives, reinforced or supported by several minimum objectives. Typically maximum objectives are likely to include:

- Receiving signed orders for major purchases

- Meeting with hard-to-see influencers or specifiers

- Presenting the solution to a problem that may have plagued the prospect

- Pinpointing opportunities upon which the prospect can capitalize.

Minimum objectives are lifesavers! Should a maximum objective slither off target, the call can still be saved. Minimum objectives represent the very least you'll accept as a result of your efforts on behalf of the prospect. They help to ensure that you don't walk away from the call empty-handed.

Though something less than earth-shaking as far as size is concerned, minimum objectives can still pay dividends. Consider these possibilities:

- Making contact with "hidden" personnel within the account who can provide valuable insights into needs, problems, or requirements not previously known

- Providing information unknown to the prospect that may affect its profits, operations, distribution patterns, or markets

- Compiling facts essential for future call preparation and execution

- Discovering the position of your competition, including strengths, acceptance, and potential.

Often what may seem to be the least of your call objectives can generate momentum in terms of new data, new ideas, and unknown requirements to which you may be able to respond. That's why it's important to note both maximum and minimum objectives in writing.

As you review your objectives prior to a call, ask yourself if they are:

- *Ambitious yet feasible?* Do they require the prospect to do something more than merely nod? How can they be phrased so that the prospect is moved to action?

- *Large enough?* Will they yield the quality of results you seek? Will they pay you well for your time? Effort?

- *Stated quantitatively?* Do they encompass precise figures? Exact amounts? Specific quantities? Percentages? Detailed applications?

- *Complementary with the prospect's?* Will they help the prospect push ahead with its objectives? Will they improve your relations with the prospect?

- *Capable of putting your competition on the defensive?* What weaknesses can they exploit? How will they strengthen your position with the prospect? What counteractions by competitors can you logically anticipate?

Objectives can be based on needs, problems, opportunities — even expectations. But until they are expressed in terms of a prospect's self-interest, there's little likelihood buying action will be triggered.

Our objective during the presentation is to create buyer *desire* for the benefits and advantages of our product or service.

A dejected young salesperson who had lost an important sale was talking with his sales manager. The rep said: "I guess it proves you can lead a horse to water, but you can't make it drink." The sales manager responded: "Let me give you a piece of advice. Your job is not to make it drink; it's to make it *thirsty.*"

Some salespeople confuse attention and interest with desire. They attempt to close the sale before the prospect fully understands how he or she will profit from the proposed action. Your prospect will buy what you present, if, and only if, he or she *wants* it. When you've made a qualified buyer "thirst" for your proposal, then you can expect a sale.

TELL THE VALUE STORY

What makes one product worth more in the eyes of the potential buyer? Successful experience with the same product is a strong factor in determining preference, but what about the prospect who has never used the product before? What are the strong motivators a salesperson can use to get across the value story?

Names make sales: Be proud of the name of the manufacturer whose products you sell. Speak it with an inflection of respect. Show how that name on the product gives it extra value and conveys the idea of leadership to whoever uses it. "It's Stueben glass." "He drives a Mercedes." People buy names that have a reputation. Talk about your company's name as though it has the aura of success about it. Imply that everyone will know the customer has the best when they see her using a product with your company's name.

Quality sells: Learn all you can about the material that goes into your product and be able to talk about its quality. Know about the material and workmanship that give your products extra value. Use success stories, test results and testimonials that prove your quality story. Show pride in your products.

Identify your product with prestige: Consumers like to buy those things that give them a better opinion of themselves and add to their prestige with others. People buy jewels not so much for personal enjoyment as for their prestige value in impressing others. When you are able to establish that owning your product is a symbol of personal pride and prestige you are appealing to a powerful buying motive.

While closely allied to the "name" value for prestige, buying and owning the product itself can have prestige and personal esteem value without a popular name attached. The office furniture salesperson, for example, can appeal to the customer's prestige value in being surrounded by new, tasteful furniture without stressing a name brand. If the brand also suggests prestige, you have a double-strength appeal.

People pay for a sense of power: The appeal of power is universal. The youngster with a beautiful new bike enjoys the power as much as the financier who buys a new shopping center. People buy books that show them how to wield more power. Computer buffs are continually upgrading simply to achieve more power, whether they really need it for their computer tasks or not.

Find the power appeal in your product. Build on the idea of the power the user will feel as he uses or contemplates its benefits. Dramatize the increase in power it will bring to the prospect's machine, or the increase in productivity it will bring to the prospect's department.

These are the four big motivators to win sales—a name that denotes success, quality, prestige and power. Tie them into your presentation and you will increase your own power and prestige through more sales!

Six basic buying motives

Buying Motive	Sales Appeal
Profit or gain	Save money, economy, profit
Fear of Loss	Safety, protection of property, health, loved ones, future security, save time, longer wear
Pleasure	Enjoyment, comfort, convenience, admiration from others, luxury, good food, housing, beauty, attractiveness, good health.
Avoidance of Pain	Relief from pain, protection, security, good health, less work, less worry.
Pride	Desire to possess, succeed, high quality, style, beauty, fashion, advance in abilities, self improvement, prestige.
Desire for Approval	Love and affection, social approval, admiration, prestige, imitation, self-improvement, sexual attraction.

CONSIDER BUYER WANTS

A psychiatrist once said that all human actions result from two basic "wants":

- The desire to enjoy a *pleasurable* experience or

- The desire to avoid a *painful* one.

Although each prospect has individual wants, or reasons for buying, they all stem from those two common sources.

As you begin a presentation, be aware that each buyer has dominant personal wants that change continuously with circumstances. To lead prospects to want the benefits of your proposal, remember they want to *enjoy pleasure* and *avoid pain*.

HOW DO YOU CREATE DESIRE?

Whether we are trying to sell a product or a course of action, we begin the presentation with two initial advantages:

- The prospect is as eager to buy profitably as you are to sell profitably.

- The prospect seeks full understanding of your product or proposal.

Here are the elements of an effective presentation:

- Present all the features and benefits of your product or proposal, if time permits. If the buyer cannot give you enough time to create sufficient desire, don't begin the presentation. Instead, arrange to see the prospect at another time. A partial presentation provides only partial understanding of your product or proposal and may even lessen a buyer's interest.

- Relate the features and benefits directly to the buyer's needs and problems.

- Appeal to those wants that are most likely to lead this prospect to buy now.

- Present the major reasons for buying *last*. When you ask for the order, you want them fresh in the prospect's mind.

ANSWER THE BUYER'S QUESTIONS

The buyer seeks to understand:

1. What's your proposal?

2. What will it do?

Generally, the buyer has broken it down into specific questions such as: "What will it do for me? for our employees? to help save money?" "How will your proposal do the things you promise? Prove it."

Even if your buyer doesn't ask these questions, you may be sure he or she is thinking them. Present clear, specific answers to even unspoken questions.

When your prospect fully understands the *features* of your proposal and the *benefits* he will gain, *desire* to enjoy the benefits follows naturally.

PRESENT FEATURES AND BENEFITS

Professional sales reps know that buyers don't buy products or proposals; they buy the benefits and advantages they will gain from taking the action you propose.

To create desire, distinguish between features and benefits:

- *Features* are unique or distinguishing characteristics or components of a product or proposal. They answer the buyer's "What is it?" question. Features are the selling points companies build into their products. If you are selling copiers, for example, the features would include number of copies per minute, collating, enlargement or reduction, color, self-stocking paper trays, and so on.

- *Benefits* are derived from the features of your product or proposal. When you present the benefits, you answer the buyer's "What will it do?" question. Benefits are *buying points*. The office manager buys copiers that will save staff time because she's responsible for total office expenses.

Thorough product knowledge is essential. As you present your product, differentiate between its features (selling points) and benefits (buying points). The buyer needs to understand both.

USE COMPARISONS

- "How does this product rate when compared with the one we're now using?"
- "What do the tests indicate?"
- "What makes you so certain we'll be better off with this one expensive version?"
- "When can we see the actual test results you've been talking about?"
- "Price-wise, how do these two items compare?"

Challenges such as these from customers demand a rapid, reasoned response. One of the surest techniques is with comparison. Being able to compare—with some degree of consistency—provides reps with a versatile and powerful sales tool. Used with discretion, comparisons also sharpen critical faculties, and allow sales reps to assess the true worth of people, products, promotions, and propositions.

In many instances it may be the only means for measuring how good or how bad a thing may be. Or distinguish the so-so from the truly extraordinary. More than that, comparisons can forecast possible problems or obstacles to sales—particularly in the areas of price, quality, and profitability. Reactions of competitors can be measured as well.

While the ground rules for making comparisons intelligently are easily understood, they are, nonetheless, demanding. Consider, for example, that for comparisons to be valid, they must be about equal in weight on both sides. Viability rests on the recognition that profound differences make comparisons neither equitable nor realistic.

Comparisons seem to work best when:

- Complete facts and data are at hand concerning the products or services to be offered.

- They are not unduly unbalanced (comparing apples and oranges, for example; or, comparing a rank amateur with an experienced professional).

- A conscious effort is made to achieve a degree of objectivity. Exaggerating a few good qualities over all other properties usually results in a failure to take other important factors into account.

- A frequent review of possible alternatives is maintained—including their influence and consequences on others.

- Possible distortions are considered that can arise from personal attitudes, prejudices, and emotions.

Comparisons play a vital role in selling. True, customers and consumers alike are constantly bombarded with a barrage of product and service contrasts. "Brand X" is frequently a target in ads, commercials and presentations at the selling level. But care must still be exercised if the comparison with your product versus the competitions' is not to be found wanting. Or worse, unbelievable.

Strong comparisons that urge customers to buy are based upon:

- Sound call planning! In addition to stressing values, benefits, and economies—review the advantages of your proposition in detail. Then, be prepared to provide proof.

- Comparing not only the strengths of your products, but their weaknesses as well. Doing so helps accounts gain a clearer perspective of what it is you are offering in the way of benefits. And it helps to stimulate a sense of trust.

- Avoid unbalanced comparisons. Reveal everything the account has a right to know. At the same time, avoid comparing with the incomparable (locomotives with hot dogs, for example)—unless it will help to identify a hidden or unique advantage or aid in changing a point of view.

- Keeping a reserve of salient features and benefits can rescue a sales situation when competitive strengths seem to be gaining the upper hand.

Comparative techniques frequently open the way to new approaches with customers that may not have been previously known. More than that, comparisons are essential to the development of a strong rapport. When backed by a sure knowledge of a customer's situation, they can be used with confidence—certain in the knowledge the call is on course.

DON'T STATE, DEMONSTRATE

You have a real advantage if you're selling a tangible product. Demonstrating is an extremely effective presentation technique.

When Pittsburgh Plate Glass introduced its unbreakable glass, one salesperson consistently outsold the rest of the sales force. The national sales manager investigated and discovered that this sales leader was literally pounding on the glass with a hammer, demonstrating to buyers that it was possible to make it shatter but impossible to break it.

Seeing is believing, and demonstration offers dramatic proof of the product's feature.

DRAMATIZING PRESENTATIONS

What does it take to make a buyer out of a prospect? There are innumerable elements, employing many skills. Drama, showmanship and creativity play crucial roles not only in capturing and holding the attention of prospects, but in selling them as well.

Why, then, is the dramatized presentation used so infrequently? And, frequently, so ineptly? Part of the reason may lie in the feeling either consciously or subconsciously that considerable genius is required to make such a presentation work. Those who refuse to consider a dramatic approach forget that it is based on a systematic, logical, step-by-step accumulation of facts and careful strategy.

A dramatic presentation isn't possible without a factual foundation. Even a genius needs something to work with. Being dramatic is more than merely communicating details, however. It expresses itself in a search for usable facts as well as in their exploitation.

To make any presentation more exciting, more compelling, more creative and more dramatic than ever before, a basic requirement must first be met: It must be different. There is no such thing as repetitive creativity. Originality is a basic factor. This fact is proven time and again in the real world of business. The salesperson who develops a unique approach...one different from that of competitors...is usually rewarded with sales success.

The problem of seizing and holding a customer's attention isn't new. Attention spans are usually short. Time is limited. Other matters press for attention. And—a salesperson's failure to realize almost any product or service has the potential for showmanship, drama, and demonstration can result in a lot of lost motion during calls.

Any time you create action, your presentation automatically becomes more interesting. Sales aids, sales tools, graphics,—even products themselves—supply the means for such action.

How do you inject drama into your presentation? Here are some tips worth testing.

- Utilize times when you are most capable of creative thinking. Begin by grouping and organizing routine chores to provide the extra thinking time needed. Then, set some idea quotas for yourself. Finally, establish deadlines.

- Make notes. Not only do they keep you from forgetting, they also aid you in the search for new possibilities, new ideas, new approaches.

- Ask creative questions. Only by questioning other peoples' thoughts and asking questions in your own mind can you hope to uncover new ideas, new combinations of thought, new dramatic appeals that will lead the way to better presentations.

  As you question ask about the which, what, and how of things.

  Ask questions about the why of things to keep yourself out of mental ruts.

Ask questions that are off-beat to keep the creative juices flowing.

Ask questions about the sales situation that will stimulate your thinking into channels that makes it possible to dramatize what it is you plan to present.

- Invent a checklist. Include in it such areas as:

Steps to take to reinforce any argument you plan to present.

Deciding what you will say, show and do to help the prospect understand what it is you are proposing.

Determining what must be done to stimulate your interest in the product or service you plan to sell.

Developing ways in which to present or demonstrate the product or service to eliminate objections.

Dramatizing ways to get the customer to say, "Okay!"

Sometimes it takes more imagination and resourcefulness to sell an idea than it did to come up with it in the first place. That's where sales tools can come in handy, provided certain cautions are observed. The first caution is also the most obvious. No matter how elaborate a sales tool may be, it isn't worth much if you are unprepared to use it. The rule-of-thumb, then, is: If you don't know, don't show!

Below is a checklist you can use to help prepare, tell and show sales tools and other dramatic devices to their best advantage.

1. What visuals, demonstration devices, media or audio equipment will you use to help clarify, amplify and dramatize your presentation?

2. What values and benefits will the sales tools selected help demonstrate for the products or services you plan to sell?

3. How can the sales tools you'll use overcome customer resistance?

4. Will they help answer questions a customer can logically be expected to ask?

5. Are the sales tools you need immediately available? In good working order: Portable? Attractive in appearance? Easily and quickly assembled?

6. How do you plan to introduce sales tools into your presentation for greatest dramatic impact?

7. What about timing? Have you practiced integrating sales tools into what you will say?

8. Should an assistant be used during your presentation to help handle any sales tools?

9. Are facilities available for effectively using your sales tools such as light switches and outlets? Shades to darken room if necessary? Have you planned for time to check them out?

10. How is your personal appearance? Does it tie in with the prestige of your product or service? What kind of an impression do you want your dress to make on the buyer?

11. What about voice tone, speed and inflection? Can you be heard clearly? Will it have a pleasant effect on the customer? Do you remember to speak a bit slower than in ordinary conversation to be better understood?

12. Are sales tools out of sight until needed? Can they be revealed on cue?

13. If printed materials will be used, be sure you are thoroughly familiar with them, and give them the emphasis they deserve.

14. Can you guide the customer in a brief thumb-through of printed materials offered. Be sure to mark copies you wish the customer to keep so that important points are easily identified for future review.

15. Will you be able to set up any visuals or audio equipment

before the presentation? Have you checked to make certain each piece of equipment is in good working order?

16. Can you keep demonstrations and other attention-attracting devices from droning along. Keep 'em short and snappy! When finished with them—get them out of the way quickly.

A dramatic presentation is more than props and gimmicks. You play a major role in its success—in the way you dress, the manner in which you speak, your sense of timing, and the tact displayed. More than that, a presentation using showmanship for dramatic effect is a compliment to customers and prospects alike. It tells them you cared enough to do the different, the unique, the unusual, yet still get across the key points of the product or service you wish to sell. It also suggests much thought and attention went into a highly personalized presentation.

FLEXIBILITY IS A KEY TO SALVAGING THE SALE

Many of the so-called "classic techniques" of salesmanship take a back seat in importance when a competitive, school-of-hard-knocks salesperson is confronted with a situation where a customer doesn't favor the product or service presented but wants something a little different.

The well-tutored expert may lose that sale if he is not flexible and able to adapt. But the gritty competitor will salvage it.

Basic flexibility may not be at the head of the list of sales attributes in training manuals, but when the time comes and it's necessary to be adaptable to save a sale, it assumes great importance.

It has been proven that one of the vital requirements for sales success is believability—whether the customer trusts the salesperson and feels the salesperson really understands the customer's situation. Assuming this believability is there, other factors, although secondary in importance, enter the scene.

One of them—never to be overlooked—is flexibility, meaning the talent to switch to a related product, or even a different approach when the first strategy hits a dead end.

Product knowledge enters in here, but what's needed goes beyond that. Something is needed in reserve. It works back to trust, also; because if the salesperson knows industry trends, attends product meetings, reads trade publications and utilizes background experience, he generates more believability due to his awareness and comprehension.

Sales reps in the building trade, for example, have long known that good selling involves solving the customer's problems, even if it means going to extreme efforts. When a salesperson is talking to an architect or builder, there's every possibility that she won't like (or can't use) the first idea presented. Then it's time to make a smooth switch to another one or a choice of alternates—one of which will capture that customer's eye.

In other fields the same is true. The customer doesn't always want something in the catalog. When it's a variation that's needed, it's no time for the salesperson to give up. Being ready to alter the presentation with regard to product appearance, size, quantity, utility or price can often redirect a challenging situation.

To attain the necessary flexibility, try to guess which variations a customer might request. Rehearse being changeable. Imagine how you'll respond to a customer's reluctance to buy your primary product. Master all your secondary products so you can promptly turn to other ideas.

Winning the confidence of the customer involves more than just generating trust. It means grappling with their problems and offering alternate solutions when this is called for. There's a lot of competition out in the field—and efforts over and above the norm are called for. Having flexibility is one way to stand out. And when your customers realize you have their best interests at heart, and will do more than your competitors to accommodate them, you can really increase your sales.

Don't Give Up Without a Fight

Life would be a lot easier if every prospect welcomed us with open arms. Sadly, that is not the case. Getting your foot in the door is usually easier than keeping it there.

Prospects have many reasons to dismiss us on the first call, such as:

- No budget
- Loyalty to your competitor
- Price too high
- Too much inventory right now
- My boss says no
- I'll think it over
- I'll call you, and so on.

I know you can add to this list. Some reasons are truthful, many are not. Prospects may not want to admit that they buy a cheaper product, or that they do not have the authority to buy. Or, the prospect may want to check you out, but doesn't want to say so.

It's a mistake not to put up a fight against this kind of buyer resistance. When you feel the buyer is insincere, is lying or not giving you the whole story, you shouldn't give up. This would be a disservice to you, your company, and probably to the prospect as well.

Regardless of how inane the reason for turning you down, and even though you know the buyer is not being truthful, you must persist, you must not give up. Remember this:

1. Don't argue
2. Be tactful
3. Don't try to steamroller
4. Don't go away mad.

You must decide whether to go on with the interview, or try again next time. Keep in mind that many buyers have trained themselves to be expert in the art of dismissal. Some are so smooth that the salesperson actually feels good about not getting the order! Watch out for these silver-tongued people.

KNOW YOUR AUDIENCE

Designing and giving presentations to prospects can be challenging, even if you're a seasoned sales pro. For example, one-on-one meetings differ significantly from group presentations. Such differences must be recognized and accommodated before, during, and after the presentation.

No matter what the size of your group, you have to be prepared when giving your presentation.

- **Identify the decision maker**. Sound obvious? Perhaps, but this is an important point that's often overlooked. Why? Because sometimes sales reps are so pleased to finally get their feet in the door that they waste time preparing a slick presentation for the wrong person or people.

  Knowing how to customize a presentation is futile if the "right one" — that is, the decision maker — is not present.

- **Differentiate the 'influencers' from the decision makers.** You may have to spend time with individuals who recommend the product or service but don't have the actual authority to make the buying decision. Those people are influencers. You'll want to design and implement a presentation that appeals to the decision maker, even if it has less appeal for the influencer.

- **Don't become too confident with the influencer.** Sometimes, if the influencer is agreeable, it's easy to become overconfident. The influencer may think you have a great product or service, and he or she may even want to go to bat for you. But there are no shortcuts — you have to get in front of the decision maker.

Don't use the influencer as a translator. Even though you may have a good relationship with the influencer, you shouldn't be wasting your time presenting to the influencer and then expecting him or her to do an effective job translating your information to the decision maker.

- **Enlist the influencer's help.** Assuming that you'll be successful in getting in front of the decision maker, you'll need to know as much as possible about this key person before you make your presentation. Ask yourself these questions: Is the decision maker concerned with the big picture? Does this person like lots of details?

  You'll need this kind of information to deliver a winning presentation, and the influencer is in the best position to give you some guidance on the decision maker's hot buttons.

Once you've ensured that you'll be presenting to the right person, your next step is to consider the size of your audience. Whether the decision maker will be your only audience member or part of a group will affect your presentation's content and organization.

In any event, you must sell yourself as a person of integrity and professional expertise. You must also sell the participants emotionally on the value of your product or service, and you must reinforce this with logic.

This will require you to rehearse every element of your presentation, so you can picture yourself in front of the group. Visualize the group by asking the influencer to describe your participants. This mental rehearsal will be invaluable.

Physically go through your presentation from beginning to end so you can be sure there are no audio or visual problems, structural confusion, or important benefits that you haven't covered.

Arrive at the meeting site at least one hour before your presentation. If possible, get into the room and double-check everything that will affect your presentation, like lights, heat, air-conditioning, projectors, extra bulbs, flip charts, markers, extension cords, and so on. Assume something could go wrong, and you will reduce the odds that it will.

Resist any inclination to apologize for not being a professional presenter. Remember, your primary objective is to sell yourself. Make your presentation exactly as you have mentally and physically rehearsed it, then ask, "Where do we proceed from here?" Stand confidently before the group and wait for a response. Usually the group will look toward the decision maker and wait for an answer from that person.

You should expect a clarification as to the decision time frame, requests for additional information, or even possibly, an immediate buying decision.

In order to become a highly paid professional salesperson, the ability to stand before a group and deliver a polished, powerful presentation is becoming increasingly important.

CONSIDER YOURSELF A PROBLEM SOLVER

Logically, you know that you're not going to convert every call into a sale. But, being human, occasionally it depresses you when you have spent a lot of time preparing for the call, and you know that your products are a fit for your prospect's business, but the prospect still doesn't buy. Sometimes you wish you could simply sell to your established accounts and just avoid calling on new prospects.

Doctors have no call reluctance because, when they see new patients, they have neither a negative nor a positive attitude. They just focus on whether the patient has a problem they can solve.

Like doctors, salespeople are problem solvers. You can't make a customer of every new prospect you see. However, if you approach the prospect with the attitude that you are a problem solver and probe to find out whether the prospect has a problem that you can solve, you cannot be rejected. If the prospect doesn't have a problem, or has one but doesn't want it solved, you haven't failed. If the prospect does want your solution to a problem, you have been successful.

When you really believe that you're calling on new accounts to see if they have problems you can solve, you'll enjoy selling a lot more. Try it! All you have to lose is your call reluctance.

IF YOU CAN'T GET THE ORDER, GET A COMMITMENT

There no need to remind any salesperson that you can't close every sale on the first call. Even after a great sales presentation, prospects have a way of refusing to buy for some reason.

In some types of selling, experience shows that a salesperson cannot afford additional calls on the same prospect. The odds are better with a fresh one. But for industrial salespeople, particularly, more than one call is the norm. If the sales potential is there, the salesperson should try to get a commitment to buy later whenever he realizes that a sale today is not in the cards.

Assuming that you have made the benefits clear and have pointed out the penalties for waiting, here are three ways to try for a commitment to buy later.

1. **Ask for a definite time.** Ask when the prospect will buy and get an appointment for that time. Avoid the appearance of high pressure by pointing out the benefits of owning the

product or service as soon as possible.

2. **Obligate the prospect to buy.** Out-deserve your competition. Do so much for the prospect that she will feel obligated to give you the order later.

3. **Give the prospect a taste of ownership.** Help the prospect visualize owning the product so she'll make an extra effort to overcome the problems. Automobile salespeople use the test drive, office machines salespeople leave a trial machine, furniture salespeople have you sit on the sofa and ask you to imagine it in your living room.

QUICK TIPS

- Prepare a plan to achieve your call objectives. Consider your strategy for each step of the presentation. Have a back-up plan.

- Assemble and organize, in a logical sequence, all the materials you expect to use during your sales presentation.

- Give some thought to what you want to say during the first few minutes after you meet the prospect. An old proverb says, "Of a good beginning cometh a good end."

- Remember the 12 BEs:
    1. Be yourself and forget yourself
    2. Be businesslike
    3. Be courteous and considerate
    4. Be neat and dress appropriately
    5. Be constantly aware of the importance of the buyer's name
    6. Be willing to listen carefully
    7. Be humble
    8. Be tolerant
    9. Be careful of your speech and grammar
    10. Be in control of the situation
    11. Be alert
    12. Be calm and poised.

WHAT WOULD YOU DO?

Your sales presentation takes at least 30 minutes, and your prospect has agreed to this time frame. Now your prospect says, "I can only give you 10 minutes." What do you do?

Is the prospect really too busy or merely stalling? Here is a simple test you can perform to find out.

Few prospects are too busy to listen to true benefits, so have a list of them ready: time savings, convenience, prestige, family welfare. If your prospect is business-minded, stress profitability: "This will make you money!"

If the prospect will not budge when you have reminded him or her of the time required to present your product, and you have done a good job of stressing benefits, it would appear that the prospect really is busy and not stalling. Perhaps at this point you will be asked to come back at a later time.

If however, you suspect that your prospect is putting you off and not really in a time bind, try a couple of final measures before setting another appointment:

- Stress the timeliness of dealing *now*. If you have a valid "buy now" option, use it:

    —"I cannot guarantee this price after (date)."

    —"Supplies are getting short. They probably won't be available after (date)."

    —"Financing terms may be subject to change."

- Try to rekindle the prospect's initial interest by romancing your product and company: "Did you know that . . . . " (Give facts of research, quality, service, company history.)

- Emphasize your professionalism: "I'm too much of a professional to try to abbreviate this and *you're* too much of a pro to allow it. Can't we take more time?"

(This is especially effective as a comeback when the prospect decides to compromise: "Well, I can give you 20 minutes.")

Finally, as a last resort, agree to come back at a later time. In doing so, carefully mark down the date and the time, once again reminding the prospect of your businesslike methods. Leave with a reminder that you will need at least 30 minutes.

SUMMARY

When calling on a prospective new account, your sales presentation will need to accommodate not only the unique needs of the account, but also the fact that you're asking the prospect to change or do something different.

Change, for most people, doesn't come easily. That's why your presentation should contain a strong and convincing argument for change. It should also make the change *easy* for the prospect.

Sometimes the buyer has to justify a change to his or her superiors. Include such justification in your presentation.

If you and your company are not known to the prospect, you'll want to spend a few minutes providing this information. Stress quality, reliability, and honesty. Talk about satisfied customers. Be specific.

Don't forget that you're selling yourself as much as you're selling your company and products. The more you can do to build trust and confidence in your prospect's mind, the better chance you have of making the sale.

Accept the fact that you won't be able to sell every prospect on the first call. Leave the door open for future calls and always close on a friendly note, whether you get an order or not.

CHAPTER 9

FOLLOW-UP AFTER THE FIRST ORDER

After you make a sale, reassure your customer that he or she has done the right thing by buying your product or service. Most people do need just a little reassurance after they buy, so that they are convinced they've acted wisely. Common doubts include:

- "Should I have spent this much?"
- "Should I have looked over the competitor's product before buying?"

- "How do I know I couldn't have gotten it cheaper somewhere else?"

- "Will this product last as long and perform as well as others?"

- "Will this company provide the service the salesperson promises?"

Before you leave your customer, make it a practice to dismiss any lingering doubts with a simple statement, such as: "I know you'll be happy with our product. You have made the right decision for your company."

Easing customer doubts

Additionally, you can employ the "sale-within-a-sale" technique by getting new customers to "reconvince" themselves they've made a good deal.

As you exit from your next successful sales call, say to your new customer: "Ms. Johnson, before I leave, I'd like to ask you a question.."

"Yes, what is it?"

"Well," you reply, putting sincerity, even humility into your voice, "I'm always trying to improve myself, so there's something I'd like to know. You've shopped around and compared prices. You're certainly aware of my competitors—and yet, you didn't buy from any of them. What was it that made you decide in favor of my proposition?"

At this point, be quiet and really listen. You're going to hear things that are invaluable to you, such as:

- "Your price was right."

- "It was a combination of a good deal and the person involved—a little of each.

- "You didn't try to sell me more than I need."

- "I've been high-pressured other places, but you never poured on the pressure."

- "You followed up when you became clear about my situation and about how your product could help me. And I like that."

- "Buying from you was a personal thing. I felt that you really cared about me. And I feel confident that, in the future, you'll continue to care about me and my needs."

Needless to say, you are listening carefully and making mental notes. After all, this is extremely valuable stuff.

In a practical sense, the more reasons this person gives for buying from you, the more she will become convinced that she has just made a "wise decision."

This kind of response means that your product is being sold all over again—this time by the customer!

How can this new account get a case of buyer's remorse at this point?

How can she want to cancel an order after listing all the wonderful reasons the just-concluded sale was such a wise decision?

But simple statements of reassurance, while important, are not all that must follow getting the customer's initial order.

Whether you've acquired new customers through company-supplied leads or your own prospecting, you now need to hover over these accounts to keep them happy — and on the books.

Here are some suggestions on how to hover:

- *Send a thank-you note.* There's something about a sincere, handwritten thank-you note that gets noticed — and remembered. Those who don't use notes excuse themselves by saying: "It's too time-consuming"; "It takes too much effort"; or "There's no payoff, so why bother?" This reasoning is shortsighted. A thank-you note may not produce immediate business, but it does produce an impression — which is invaluable in the long run. A handwritten message prompts a customer to think: "I appreciate the fact that this salesperson thinks enough about me and my business to write that note."

• *Make sure the first delivery goes well.* The first delivery to a new account is pivotal in solidifying a good customer relationship. This is a time to cement the emerging relationship with an expression of concern and gratitude. It's also a prime opportunity to make a favorable impression with many people you haven't previously met during the selling steps.

Delivery is the beginning of many customer "service" calls. They are designed to guarantee customer satisfaction, control the flow of profitable repeat orders, and open opportunities for additional sales to other departments and divisions of the account.

The first delivery may require the installation of the product. For example, in the office equipment industry, the purchased products are delivered, set up, and demonstrated to the employees.

Usually, the salesperson's service technician will carefully show the employees how to operate the new equipment. The sales rep and service tech team sets the stage for good customer service relations. Like the salesperson, the service tech should be well-versed in customer relations. Repair techniques play an important part in repeat supply business — and additional equipment orders.

Execute the delivery of the first order just as carefully as the initial sales call. Remember that all calls on the account, both before and after the sale, should be carefully planned.

Your personal impact, service, and careful handling of details will help you control and maintain the important business you have captured.

- *Take care of problems immediately.* This is the time to show empathy. The customer wants to know that you care as much about solving the emergency as he or she does. When a new customer reports some kind of difficulty, you must take action *today*, not tomorrow. Listen to the problem, give the customer the benefit of the doubt, and decide on a solution. Your ability to respond quickly and efficiently will be remembered much more vividly than the complaint.

  Dragging your feet in such a situation — even if a customer complaint catches you at the worst time — is a mistake. Making it your business to fix any customer problems will pay off many times over in the future.

- *Phone customers back immediately.* Don't view returning phone calls as secondary in importance to the moment's wheeling and dealing. Falling into the "I'll do it when I get around to it" syndrome is hazardous to the health of future sales! Waiting for a couple of days to return calls is the wrong strategy. If you really want to build a healthy customer base, you have to return phone calls right away. Doing so is a key building block of your success.

- *Stick to every promise.* Your new customer says: "Make sure this item is included," or "Double-check to make sure this detail is taken care of." If you reply: "You can count on me," then you'd better live up to your word! Whenever you make a promise, remember that your future business with this customer depends upon the quality of your follow-through.

This is an opportunity to show genuine interest in the long-term needs of your customer. It's a time to reflect on the steps you can take to ensure that future needs are met.

• *Stay in close touch.* Make regular phone calls and, whenever possible, personal visits. Letters and mailing pieces just can't do the complete job. They're hardly adequate when a customer wants to see you personally because he or she has a gripe, needs an important question answered, or is being wooed by a competitor!

When the customer invites you to come in and talk about a problem or make a special presentation, it's a sign that the customer is looking for progressive, strategic thinking on your part. This is the ideal time to show your creativity.

Staying involved with your customer is the only way to stay on top of the things you need to know.

VIEW FROM THE CATBIRD'S SEAT

It might be instructive to hear the buyer's point of view.

Andrew Schrank is the manager of transportation operations for Freightliner Corporation. And he will not tolerate reps who aren't responsive to his needs. He says, "A lot of salespeople will tell you just about anything to get your business. It's *keeping* the business that's important."

Schrank expects salespeople to have:

1. *A firsthand knowledge of how their own companies operate.* Schrank likes salespeople who have operations experience and who "understand freight flow from their own hands-on experience."

2. *An in-depth knowledge of their prospect's business.* Schrank wants salespeople who know what Freightliner does, who

its customers and suppliers are, where the company's production levels are now, and where they are projected to be in the future. To demonstrate the importance of on-time service to his company, he gives salespeople special plant tours.

3. *The time to explain how their own companies operate.* Schrank expects salespeople to keep Freightliner updated on any changes in their operations, including driver shortages, on-time performance problems, and the like.

4. *A good rapport with their own operating people.* Schrank demands that salespeople work well with the people in their organizations who can get things done.

5. *A strong interest in providing dependable follow-up.* Schrank is impressed by salespeople who grasp problems, take ownership of them, communicate about them with total honesty, follow up on them, and present viable solutions.

While it isn't always possible to provide salespeople who have prior operating experience in the fields in which their products or services are used, it is certainly reasonable to expect that sales reps know exactly what their products will be used for and how they will benefit their customers.

Reps who are persistent in getting to know a prospect's business are persistent in getting to know people who can help that prospect's business. At any given time, you might be trying to get to know a variety of people within a firm — a purchasing agent, an end user, a business committee member, or a manager. The more people you get to know, the more opportunities you'll have to clinch the sale — and the more likely these people will be to remember you as someone who will "beat the bushes" for them.

As you're making the rounds of a prospect's business, let people know that you'll keep abreast of their colleagues, their competition, and their industry. Let them know that you're willing to meet people far and wide on their behalf: to get answers to questions, to exchange industry information, and to search out solutions to problems.

It is also reasonable to expect that sales professionals will be advocates for their customers. Customers want to know that their sales reps will speak on their behalf to sales managers, product managers, and manufacturers. They want to know that you have the gumption to smash through bureaucracy to get their questions answered and their problems resolved.

Let your customer know you'll communicate with your superiors on the customer's behalf as vigorously as you pursue a sale.

QUICK TIPS

- You are part of the package you offer your customer. When an account places its faith in you and your company, it means you've generated trust. The account is buying you as much as the product — perhaps more so.

- Demonstrate your skills when problems develop. Next time a customer approaches you with a problem or complaint, look at it as an opportunity to demonstrate your efficiency. Let your customer see that you won't rest until the problem is resolved to his or her satisfaction.

- Always send a personal thank-you letter immediately after the sale.

- Return calls promptly whenever customers report problems.

- Invite customers to tour your facilities.

- If possible, be present for product delivery and setup following the initial sale.

- Call to ensure that the product is working exactly as expected.

- Call occasionally to check if your customer needs product parts, repairs, and the like.

- Keep your new customer informed of industry news and other items of interest.

WHAT WOULD YOU DO?

Because of a foul-up in our shipping department, one of my new customers failed to receive her order. The buyer is angry and suggests that this may be both my first and last order. What's the best way to handle this?

Your customer is angry, and with good reason. In situations like this, you must act fast to assure the customer that the order foul-up will not happen again.

First, find out what caused the problem and do what needs to be done to see that the problem will not be repeated.

Second, visit the customer as soon as possible, and be empathetic. *Listen.* Let the customer say whatever she wants to say. Don't interrupt.

When your customer finishes, say something like, "I've looked into this matter, and here's what I (or my company) have done to see that it absolutely will not happen again." After describing what you have done, tell the customer how much you value her business.

This is not the time to mention why the customer would be making a mistake to switch to another supplier or to go into a presentation on why your products or services are so much better.

DO'S AND DON'TS

Do:

- Solve the problem before the call
- Get to the customer quickly
- Listen
- Be empathetic
- Show that you understand
- State how much you value your customer's business.

Don't:

- Say, "It's not my fault"
- Denigrate your own people
- Overapologize
- Create a bigger problem
- Give a major pitch for your products.

SUMMARY

All your work prospecting, then working hard and long to get the first order can be all for nothing if the customer is not happy. That's why following up after the first order is so important.

If you follow the procedures suggested in this chapter, you should have a very high new-customer retention rate.

Some salespeople actually follow first orders through their own order processing, shipping, and billing departments to see that nothing goes wrong. They're either at the customer's receiving point when the delivery is made, or they're on the phone with the customer's warehouse or store receiving person at about the time the shipment should be arriving.

If they're selling a service, they're in touch with the individuals receiving that service and monitoring it through to completion. Literally nothing can fall between the cracks with these professional salespeople.

And they don't stop there. They continue to keep a careful watch on all aspects of customer service on the second order, and beyond.

The days of "sell 'em and leave 'em" are long gone. The days of exceptional customer service are here. And there's no time that it's more important than after the first order.

Connecting With Your Customers is a step-by-step guide that teaches you the communication skills essential for forging a trusting, understanding relationship with a potential customer. Let this practical, pertinent program provide you with the latest sales communication information. It is your key to sales mastery. It is your key to ultimate success.
278 Pages; Hardcover; $28.95

THE IDEA-A-DAY GUIDE TO SUPER SELLING AND CUSTOMER SERVICE
BY TONY ALESSANDRA, PH.D., GARY COUTURE, AND GREGG BARON

The Idea-A-Day Guide is packed with practical, money-making ideas — one for every working day of the year — that will increase your selling power. This is a one-of-a-kind source for new ways to boost productivity, manage accounts, approach customers, make presentations, and close more sales. More than 100 work sheets help you plan, test, and execute new skills. Whether you have been in sales for 20 days or 20 years, you'll have an easy-to-use, daily reference for getting a new idea or even reminding yourself of effective ideas you have heard about or used before.
310 Pages; Paperback; $19.95

MORE THAN A FOOT IN THE DOOR
$12.95   Book code: 8137

CLOSE IT RIGHT, RIGHT NOW!
$12.95   Book code: 8138

DO YOU HAVE ANY OBJECTIONS?
$12.95   Book code: 8139

185 SALES TIPS FOR SURE-FIRE SUCCESS
$21.50   Book code: 1233

10 STEPS TO CONNECTING WITH YOUR CUSTOMERS
$28.95   Book code: 1032

THE IDEA-A-DAY GUIDE TO SUPER SELLING AND CUSTOMER SERVICE
$19.95   Book code: 1185

BILL MY: ❑ VISA   ❑ AMERICAN EXPRESS   ❑ MASTERCARD   ❑ COMPANY

CARD NUMBER _____ EXP. DATE _____

NAME_____ TITLE_____

COMPANY _____

ADDRESS _____

CITY/STATE/ZIP _____

SIGNATURE _____ PHONE_____

(Signature and phone number are necessary to process order.)   95-5509

❑ Please send me your latest catalog

Copies may be ordered from your bookseller or from Dartnell.

To order from Dartnell, call toll free **(800) 621-5463** or fax us your order **(800) 327-8635**

D A R T N E L L
4660 N RAVENSWOOD AVE CHICAGO IL 60640-4595 PHONE: (800) 621-5463 or FAX: (800) 327-8635